Flowering Potted Plants

Prolonging Shelf Performance

Grateful acknowledgement is given to Thomas J. Sheehan for his pronunciations in this book, and UF, Aalsmeer, AFE.

Also, grateful acknowledgement for photos is given to Ball Seed Co., especially Will Healy and Lisa Segroves; B. L. Cobia, Inc. for Rhipsalidopsis heather and Schlumbergera Christmas Fantasy; Marc Cathey; August De Hertogh for Amadeus freesia; Goldsmith Seeds, Inc. for Sierra liliac; GrowerTalks magazine; Hatten's Nursery for Bougainvillea; Netherlands Flower Bulb Information Center for crocus, Hippeastrum amaryllis, Muscan grape hyacinthus, Tête à Tête narcissus, oxalis and Orange Monarch tulip, and PanAmerican Seed Co.

Cover photo courtesy Goldsmith Seeds, Inc.

Flowering Potted Plants

Prolonging Shelf Performance

Postproduction Care & Handling

Terril A. Nell

Ball Publishing

Batavia, Illinois USA

Ball Publishing
335 North River Street
P.O. Box 9
Batavia, IL 60510-0009 USA

Printed in the United States of America

98 97 96 95 94 93   5 4 3 2 1

Library of Congress Cataloging in Publication Data

Nell, T.A. (Terril A.)
  Flowering potted plants : prolonging shelf performance :
  postproduction care & handling / Terril A. Nell.
      p. cm.
  Includes bibliographical references and index.

  ISBN 0-9626796-8-2 : $42.00.
  1. Plants, Potted—Handling.   2. Flowers—Handling.
  3. Plants, Potted—Postharvest technology.
  4. Flowers—Postharvest techology.   I. Title.
  SB442.5.N44 1993   92-45173
  635.9'866—dc20   CIP

CONTENTS

Other flowering plant possibilities

Glossary   93

Crop Index   95

FOREWORD

*F*lowering Potted Plants: Prolonging Shelf Performance is one of a series of books about the care and handling of plants from grower to consumer. It's designed to give the entire marketing-user chain of grower, wholesaler, retailer and consumer the current recommendations on the most effective procedures for each postproduction stage—as each has its own specific considerations.

Today, many plants can be grown especially for display in interior spaces when the growing media, water, nutrients and pest control measures are adjusted for interior culture. Flowering potted plants have benefited from extensive advances in breeding, culture chemicals and new transportation practices. We have the knowledge to ensure potted plants continued success throughout the year. All of these significant developments have added a broader list of plants to use, a longer season of availability for purchase and performance, and greater flexibility in the successful management of container-grown flowering plants. This guide deals with the specific requirements for the postproduction care and handling of container-grown plants. We hope you will find the successful practice of postproduction care begins here.

The Postproduction series includes the following four books: *Bedding Plants: Prolonging Shelf Performance* by Allan M. Armitage, University of Georgia; *Cut Flowers: Prolonging Freshness* by John N. Sacalis, Rutgers University, and edited by Joseph L. Seals; *Flowering Potted Plants: Prolonging Shelf Performance* by Terril A. Nell, University of Florida; and *Foliage Plants: Prolonging Quality* by Thomas M. Blessington, University of Maryland, and Pamela C. Collins, landscape design and interior plantscaping consultant.

These four postproduction books originated from the series produced through the Kiplinger Chair in Horticulture at The Ohio State University, Columbus, OH. During 1980-1981, I occupied the Kiplinger Chair, which is funded by businesses, foundations and individuals to support research and educational activities for floricultural excellence. The Chair honors Dr. D.C. Kiplinger, professor of floriculture, for his contributions as a teacher, researcher and extension specialist.

Recommendations for the Chair urged expanded research in production and distribution of high quality floral products, and postproduction books on bedding plants, cut flowers, flowering potted plants and foliage plants were subsequently planned and produced by the Kiplinger Chair.

Committee members during the creation of the guides were: Stanley F. Backman, Minneapolis, MN; Roger D. Blackwell, Columbus, OH; H. Marc Cathey, Beltsville, MD; for the Ohio Florists Association: Willard H. Barco, Medina, OH, James F. Bridenbaugh, Kent, OH, and August J. Corso, Sandusky, OH; Paul Ecke Jr., Encinitas, CA; Harry K. Tayama, Columbus, OH; and for The Ohio State University: Robert A. Kennedy, Steven M. Still and Luther Waters Jr.

H. Marc Cathey
National Chair for Florist
 and Nursery Crops Review
U.S. Department of Agriculture
Washington, DC

INTRODUCTION

Annual sales of flowering potted plants keep setting new records as the popularity of these crops continues to soar among American consumers. Commercial flower growers are responding to demands from retail florists and mass markets year-round, not just during traditional holiday periods. And the introduction of new plants offering more flower colors, plant forms and interior uses has significantly broadened the range of choices available today compared to the past. Successful marketing of high-quality, long-lasting plants motivates consumers to take advantage of opportunities to purchase plants for household use, gifts and special occasions.

Flowering plants are now being shipped considerable distances, from the point of production to locations throughout the United States, requiring that plants be sleeved and properly handled to maintain plant quality and to optimize lifespan. In addition, the rapid growth of the U.S. interiorscape industry has resulted in flowering potted plants being utilized in locations that may provide less than optimum conditions. The longevity and postproduction quality of flowering potted plants will be the primary considerations in the selection and continued increased sales of these products.

The quality of flowering potted plants at the time of sale—as evaluated by plant size, flower color and size, plant form, leaf color and the absence of blemishes due to mechanical damage and insect or disease infestation—is determined by the grower and is directly affected by environmental conditions and cultural practices used in production. However, postproduction quality and longevity is dependent on the production practices and the handling procedures used by the shipper, retailer and consumer. The relative impact that each segment of the industry has on longevity is not known and can never be fully established since many factors affect the ultimate lifespan of flowering potted plants. It's known that a poorly produced plant cannot be improved by the most carefully designed handling procedures, but longevity of a high-quality plant can decline rapidly if not cared for properly. Therefore, it's vital that the environmental conditions, handling procedures and cultural practices affecting longevity be recognized by the industry and that this knowledge be used to maximize the life of the flowering potted plants for the consumer.

The information contained in this manual has been developed from research results from the United States and Europe. Every effort has been made to include all published information and to recognize individuals who have conducted this work with citations at the end of each crop outline. Individuals seeking additional information on specific crops are encouraged to refer to these references for more details.

POSTPRODUCTION FACTORS

Cultivar

The value of cultivar selection in improving interior performance of flowering potted plants has not been emphasized in the past. Cultivar differences, such as flower color, number of flowers and time to flowering, have been used as industrywide criteria in evaluating new cultivars. These are important factors and should continue to be used to assess new cultivars. In addition, however, the tolerance of each cultivar to shipping conditions, low interior light levels, ethylene and chilling must also be included in our future evaluations.

Significant differences exist in the postharvest longevity of nearly all flowering potted plant species on the market today. It's known that poinsettia cultivars differ in their response to sleeving, as evidenced by the presence of leaf and bract droop after sleeves are removed. Also, many of the most commonly produced chrysanthemum cultivars have relatively short interior longevities. Clearly, the selection of a cultivar that is more tolerant of adverse shipping conditions and suboptimal interior conditions is the easiest way to assure that a quality plant is provided to customers. In this manual, known longevity differences among cultivars and/or differences following shipping are highlighted, but research work in this area is sketchy and additional investigation is needed.

Development stage

Flowering plants are sold for the colorful appearance of the blooms and, in most cases, plants are sold with sufficient flower color or numbers of flowers open to give the consumer a good idea of the ultimate appearance. The maturity of flowering potted plants at marketing is a major factor in the successful interior performance of these plants. Flowering plants placed in the interior before flower color has fully developed (unripe) generally develop pale flower color indoors. The development of light-colored flowers indoors is a serious problem on plants having multiple flowers, such as cineraria, calceolaria, or those which continue to flower indoors, such as hibiscus. It's important that plants have good flower color before the plant is sold.

Harvesting plants at the bud stage has become a valuable procedure with cut flowers, but this practice can be a disaster for many flowering potted crops. On the other hand, plants can be sold too mature (ripe). For instance, poinsettias should be fully colored at the time of sale, but leaf and bud drop are greater once the plants are moved indoors if they are sold after the cyathia are open. Chrysanthemums, however, if sold before the flowers are half open, will develop pale flower color and reduced flower size indoors.

It must be emphasized that the stage of marketability depends on the time required to get the plant to market. Plants being shipped long distances should be sold at a less mature stage than those for local market sales. Most plants with many open flowers are more difficult to ship, are more sensitive to ethylene (discussed below), and are damaged more easily after they leave the production area than plants that are shipped with buds showing color or that have few open flowers. Shipping plants with open flowers is a problem with hibiscus, Easter lilies, Christmas cacti, Regal geraniums and others, while it is not a problem for poinsettias or chrysanthemums. Clearly, the proper development stage for marketing is variable, but its importance cannot be overlooked. It's one of the major methods that commercial producers can use to maintain crop quality once the plant is sold.

Temperature

Production temperatures should be lowered during the production cycle's final 2 to 3 weeks to enhance the flower color and increase the plant's stored carbohydrate levels which may lead to increased longevity. Temperatures should not be reduced to levels that will lead to chilling injury on sensitive plants. Reductions of 2° to 3°F during the final weeks of production may cause "pinking" (development of pink petal edges) on some white cultivars, such as chrysanthemums. Summer-produced (high temperature) plants have been reported to have a shorter shelf life than winter-produced (cool temperature) plants.

Light

Optimum light levels, as required for each crop, must be maintained to produce plants with good interior longevity, maximum number of flowers, good leaf development, good flower color and proper height without excessive stretching. Suboptimal light levels lead to premature bud abscission in poinsettias and to reduced longevity in chrysanthemums. Reduced light level during the entire crop cycle or during the final weeks of production has been a valuable acclimatization technique for foliage plants, but it's of no value in flowering potted plants and may cause reduced longevity.

Medium

Effects of various media components and the relationship of root development to longevity have not been identified at the present time. It's clear that a porous medium that can be easily rewetted by the consumer and interiorscaper is vital to the optimum performance of flowering plants indoors. A number of polymer gels have been developed to be used to maintain a moist medium and keep the plant from drying out in the interior. Unfortunately, no evaluations have been conducted with these gels under interior conditions. Manufacturers' literature suggests that watering may be delayed 20% to 40% when these materials are incorporated into the medium before planting. Under interior conditions, this could mean that watering would be delayed 4 to 8 hours on some of the high-water-use flowering plants such as hydrangea, chrysanthemum and poinsettia. At present, some interiorscapers and mass market buyers have decided that the slight delay in watering does not justify the additional cost of adding these gels to the medium. Irrigation with a wetting agent at the time of marketing has been valuable as a means of allowing the medium to be easily rewetted.

Fertilization

The nutritional program and fertilization practices may have more effect on flowering potted plants' longevity than any other cultural procedure. Fertilization practices to consider are elemental ratios, fertilization concentration and the time at which fertilization is discontinued during the crop cycle. The ratio of ammonia (including urea) to nitrate nitrogen should be approximately 40% ammonia and 60% nitrate. These ratios prevent ammonia toxicity problems and increase interior longevity for the plants where evaluations have been made. Elemental ratios are important to prevent antagonistic restrictions of certain elements. Most commercial fertilizer formulations provide good nutrient balances.

It had been suggested for a number of years that the nitrogen:potassium ratio be maintained at 1:1 until about 3 weeks before flowering, when it can be changed to a 0.5:1 ratio. Recent research has failed to demonstrate any benefit from changing this ratio on potted chrysanthemums. It may be beneficial to switch to a 100% nitrate nitrogen during the final weeks of production, but this has not been evaluated at the present time. One recent finding that has proven to have a major effect on potted mums, azaleas and possibly other crops is the termination of fertilizer during the final 3 weeks of production. Chrysanthemum longevity can be extended by 7 to 14 days with this procedure, depending on the fertilizer concentration, cultivar and time of year. The overall fertilization program should be carefully developed to assure the production of high-quality plants with optimal longevity.

Shipping temperature and duration

Maintaining proper shipping temperatures and keeping shipping durations short are two of the best ways to assure that high-quality plants leaving the production area will arrive at the retail store in good condition and exhibit good lasting qualities. Plants subjected to transit stress will exhibit characteristic symptoms, such as leaf yellowing and drop and flower bud drop. These problems may be due to exposure to ethylene during shipping, sensitivity to darkness or high respiration rates due to elevated shipping temperatures which lead to rapid carbohydrate depletion. Some new European information suggests the use of a red light source during shipping to reduce the detrimental effects of darkness (leaf drop) during shipping. This procedure has no application in the United States at the present time; however, since plants shipped for long distances are packed in closed boxes, the light wouldn't reach the plants.

Shipping and storage temperatures should be maintained from 40° to 60°F (4° to 16°C)

for flowering potted plants, with specific temperatures dependent on plant species. Chilling-sensitive plants, such as African violets, poinsettias and hibiscus, should be shipped or held above 50°F (10°C). Temperatures above 60° to 62°F (16° to 17°C) will lead to greater and more rapid leaf and flower abscission and leaf yellowing. The optimum shipping temperatures for a wide range of flowering potted plants are included with each crop in the manual.

Sensitivity to gases

Numerous gases may affect the longevity, interior appearance and performance of flowering potted plants indoors. One of the most damaging is ethylene, an odorless and colorless gas that is produced by plant materials and is a byproduct of combustible engines. A large number of flowering plants are sensitive to very low ethylene concentrations (less than 100 parts per billion) even when exposure times are 2 to 4 hours or less. The degree of injury depends on the plant species, ethylene concentration, duration of exposure and temperature at the time the plants are exposed. The symptoms of ethylene injury include leaf, bud and flower drop; rapid flower aging and wilting; epinasty (drooping of leaves and bracts); increased microbial attack; and flower/bud abortion. Because ethylene exposure can make high-quality crops unmarketable, it's of considerable interest to the entire floriculture industry to develop techniques to reduce ethylene sensitivity.

One of the most effective ways is to reduce shipping temperatures. Many flowering plants will not exhibit ethylene exposure symptoms at shipping temperatures of 40°F (4°C), while leaf yellowing and bud drop will occur at 60°F (16°C). Of course, this procedure cannot be used on chilling-sensitive crops.

Another procedure in commercial use is the foliar application of silver thiosulfate (STS) to potted flowering plants. STS acts as an antagonist to ethylene and reduces

15

ethylene production in the flowers, minimizing the detrimental effects of ethylene exposure. Application of STS has had mixed results on ethylene-sensitive potted plants. Petal shattering was reduced significantly on geraniums, but plants were then very sensitive to root rot organisms. Work in the United States and Europe has shown that STS reduces hibiscus bud drop most of the time. The variation obtained with STS applications is probably a result of improper chemical mixing procedures, incorrect rate or improper time of application. It must also be understood that STS application will not overcome the effects of improper shipping temperatures. In many flowering potted plants, it's necessary to apply STS just as the buds begin to enlarge rather than at time of marketability. Application at flowering has not been effective on some crops.

Work is underway in the United States and Europe to identify the procedures for effective use of STS on flowering potted plants. Be aware that local ordinances may restrict the use of STS, since one of the primary components—silver—is a heavy metal. For example, STS spray applications are prohibited in Holland. Overall, STS has been a valuable means of minimizing the harmful effects of ethylene, and it should be considered for sensitive crops.

Interior light level

Most flowering potted plants will develop the largest number of flowers with good flower color under high interior light conditions. Of course, the light response is crop-dependent and varies by temperature. Poinsettias lose fewer leaves at light levels of 100 fc (1.1 klux) or higher and hibiscus lose fewer buds at 400 fc (4.3 klux) than at 100 fc (1.1 klux). Hibiscus will drop all buds within a week indoors and cease to flower if placed at 20 fc (215 lux), the light level required to maintain flowering on an African violet. Generally, however, these crops (including crops requiring low light like

African violet) will develop best as the light level is increased, but avoid direct sunlight.

There are exceptions. No differences have been found in the interior longevity of azaleas placed at 25 to 100 fc (.3 to 1.1 klux), although differences in flower color and overall quality have been observed at low light levels. Similarly, interior light level has little effect on the postharvest longevity of bulbous crops, but flower color is enhanced and flower stalks don't elongate as much at high light levels as at low light levels.

Interior temperature

All flowering potted plants will last longer if maintained at cooler temperatures, but the exact temperature for optimum performance is crop-dependent. For instance, potted bulbs, calceolaria, cineraria and cyclamen will do fine at 55° to 60°F (13° to 16°C), and longevity will be excellent. The lifespan of these crops is reduced significantly at warmer temperatures, especially temperatures above 75° to 80°F (24° to 27°C). More temperature-tolerant crops, such as chrysanthemum, will last as long at 75°F (24°C) as a potted tulip will last at 60°F (16°C). Because of the effect that high temperatures have on flower longevity, it's advised that retailers, interiorscapers and consumers place plants at the temperatures suggested in this manual to obtain maximum longevity.

Interior temperature will affect the crop in ways other than longevity. Flowering plants placed at 80°F (27°C), for instance, will generally have lighter flower colors, increased stem (stalk) length, rapid leaf yellowing and leaf drop. Flowering poinsettias placed at 25 fc (269 lux) and 65°F (18°C) will lose few leaves over a 30-day period. However, the same poinsettia cultivar maintained at the same light level, but with the temperature increased to 80°F (27°C), will lose nearly all of its leaves over that same period.

Irrigating

It's vital that plants don't dry out indoors—failure to water a flowering potted plant properly indoors and allowing it to wilt decreases postharvest longevity. On the other hand, overwatering leads to root injury and rapid plant decline. Plants should be kept uniformly moist at all times. Ideally, instructions would include clear guidelines for watering, such as to water plants every day or every 2 days. However, strict guidelines are impossible due to the wide variation of indoor light levels, temperatures and humidities. Of course, plant size and growing medium will influence watering frequency. Larger plants will require more frequent watering than smaller ones of the same cultivar. Water should be applied to the medium without wetting the flowers or foliage and should not be allowed to stand in the bottom of a container for longer than 30 minutes. Subirrigation (controlled watering) containers provide an excellent system to maintain uniform moisture and avoid wetting of the flowers and foliage.

Many flowering potted plants have high water requirements, especially during the first week indoors. Several materials have been introduced as a means of reducing water requirements (antitranspirants) or to provide a larger reservoir of water in the medium (polymer gels). Antitranspirants are sprayed on foliage either to cover stomates chemically or to close the stomates as a means of reducing water loss. Several of these materials have not been shown to reduce water loss appreciably on hydrangeas and cineraria under interior conditions. In addition, some injury to flowers or bracts were noted on these crops. On foliage plants, it was found that 65% of the moisture lost indoors was from the soil medium rather than through the foliage, which may explain the minimal value of antitranspirants on flowering potted plants. Presently, no strong benefit of the materials indoors has been identified.

The benefit from using hydrophilic polymer gels in the growing medium to decrease the frequency of watering is extremely variable, and in many cases, the information is conflicting. Recent information indicates that the water-absorption capability of gels is lowered by the addition of fertilizer salts. No difference was observed in time-to-wilt when a commercial gel was incorporated into the growing medium. Thus, it's doubtful that any benefit will be realized in terms of increased water-holding capacity and decreased time-to-wilt on floriculture crops produced with standard fertilization practices.

Questions concerning the effect of water quality on longevity are unfortunately a matter for speculation at this time. Although water quality has been shown to have a significant effect on cut flower longevity, no research has explored a similar relationship on flowering pot plants.

Conclusion

Many factors affect the interior longevity of flowering potted plants. Proper production practices must be combined with good handling procedures, optimum shipping temperatures and good interior environmental conditions if flowering potted plants are to achieve their maximum performance in the interior. Careful attention to the specific requirements at each level of handling can only lead to greater consumer satisfaction and increased sales of floriculture crops in the future.

CROPS

Begonia ✕ *hiemalis*

beh-*goh*-nee-uh
he-*mal*-iss

Family Name: **Begoniaceae**
Common Names: **Hiemalis Begonia, Elatior Begonia, Rieger Begonia**

Over 1,000 species in tropics and subtropics of both hemispheres. Monoecious herbs or shrubs, usually perennial, fibrous-rooted, rhizomatous, tuberous or bulbous. *B.* ✕ *hiemalis* is a group of winter-flowering begonias derived from crossing *B. socotrana* with various Andean tuberous species or with *B.* ✕ *tuberhybrids* cvs. These combine the winter-flowering habit of *B. socotrana* and the large, colorful flowers of the Andean tuberous begonias. There are many named cultivars with single or double flowers of white, pink, red, orange or yellow.

CONNIE

Production factors

No information is available on the effects of production light level, temperature or media on the interior longevity of Hiemalis begonias.

Nutrition. High levels of fertilization result in leaf necrosis, reduced numbers of flowers and decreased interior longevity.

Development stage. Market plants when approximately 20% of the flowers are open. Buds showing color will develop indoors if given adequate light levels. New flower buds will also develop under good interior conditions.

Problems. Diseases: Powdery mildew, Botrytis.

Insects: Aphids, cyclamen mites and foliar nematodes.

Postproduction factors

Shipping, handling and storage

Light. Plants will tolerate 6 to 9 days of darkness during shipping and storage if temperatures are properly maintained.

Temperature. Ship plants at 51° to 53°F (11° to 12°C) for a duration of 3 to 5 days. Because Hiemalis begonias are cold sensitive, avoid storage and shipping temperatures below 50°F (10°C).

Gases. Avoid even short periods of ethylene exposure, or flowers and flower buds will drop. Ethylene will not damage foliage.

Begonia x hiemalis

beh-*goh*-nee-uh
he-*mal*-iss

Lasting qualities. Elatior begonias are excellent interior plants and will last 3 to 4 weeks or longer.

Care and grooming. Remove damaged leaves and flowers before storage and shipping. Plants will withstand shipping best if they are staked—unless well-branched, compact varieties are used.

Retail handling

Light. Display plants at light levels of 50 to 100 fc (.5 to 1.1 klux).

Temperature. Maintain display temperatures from 65° to 75°F (18° to 24°C). Avoid temperatures below 50°F (10°C) and above 80°F (27°C).

Irrigation. Keep plants moist but not overly wet. Drying out may cause bud drop.

Disorder. Plants have a tendency to break if they are not staked before shipping or during handling.

Consumer care

Light. Hiemalis begonias will tolerate a wide range of interior light levels, but avoid direct sunlight. Plants placed at 100 fc (1.1 klux) will continue to flower for 6 to 8 weeks, while those maintained at 25 fc (270 lux) will last only 2 to 3 weeks.

Temperature. Maintain plants at temperatures of 65° to 75°F (18° to 24°C).

Location. Choose an east or south window.

Irrigation. Overwatering can be a major problem with these plants. Keep them moist at all times but avoid overwatering and drying out.

Grooming. Remove individual flowers as they become faded.

Cultivars. Numerous cultivars are available, offering flower colors of white, pink, red, orange and yellow. Single- and double-flowered cultivars are grown in Europe and the United States. No information on longevity differences among cultivars is available.

ADDITIONAL READING

Hoyer, L. 1985. Bud and flower drop in Begonia elatior Sirene caused by ethylene and darkness. *Acta Horticultura* 167:387-391.

Larson, R.A. 1980. Begonias. *Introduction to Floriculture.* New York: Academic Press Inc.

Sterling, E.P. and W.H. Molenaar. 1985. *Transport tolerantie van potplanten. Mededeling Nr. 39.* Wageningen, The Netherlands: Sprenger Institute.

Woltering, E.J. 1987. Effects of ethylene on ornamental pot plants: a classification. *Scientia Horticultura* 31:283-294.

B

Bougainvillea spectabilis boo-gan-*vil*-lee-uh spek-*tah* bi-lis

Also: ***B. peruviana, B. x buttiana***
Family Name: **Nyctaginaceae**
Common Name: **Bougainvillea**

Originated in Brazil—perhaps 14 species of shrubs, vines or small trees in South America, usually armed with spines. Cultivated kinds are grown as woody vines but may be trained as standards in the open in far southern areas and in northern greenhouses. Bougainvillea are grown as pot plants in cool greenhouses in the North or in the South with proper photoperiod and temperature controls.

BOUGAINVILLEA

Problems. Problems have been encountered in producing uniform flowering on potted plants year-round. Many of these difficulties have been overcome through photoperiod manipulation (use of short days) and use of growth regulators.

Disease: Botrytis.

Insects: Aphids and thrips.

Postproduction factors

Shipping, handling and storage

Light. The effect of light on flower and leaf drop becomes evident after extended shipping and storage periods. Plants remaining in closed boxes for longer than 3 days will drop flowers and bracts, even at optimum temperatures.

Temperature. Bougainvillea, a native of tropical areas in Brazil, is sensitive to chilling during storage and transport. Avoid temperatures below 50°F (10°C), or flowers

Production factors

No information is available on the effects of production light, temperature or media on bougainvillea longevity.

Development stage. Market plants when 25% to 50% of the bracts are fully colored.

Bougainvillea spectabilis boo-gan-*vil*-lee-uh spek-*tah* bi-lis

and leaves will drop, the severity depending on duration of exposure to these temperatures. Provide shipping temperatures of 55° to 60°F (13° to 16°C) for optimum performance.

Gases. Plants are sensitive to ethylene, with exposure causing flower and bract drop. Apply silver thiosulfate to reduce this problem. However, since this treatment is not totally effective, exposure to ethylene should be avoided.

Lasting qualities. Plants will last 21 to 30 days under interior conditions and can then be used outdoors as patio plants after flowering has ceased indoors. Additional flowers will develop on the new growth.

Care and grooming. Water plants well 12 to 24 hours before boxing. Remove damaged or diseased leaves and flowers before storage and shipping to retail markets.

Retail handling

Light. Display plants in areas providing light levels of 100 fc (1.1 klux) or higher for best results. Avoid displaying plants in direct sunlight since they may dry out rapidly.

Temperature. Maintain optimum display temperatures from 70° to 80°F (21° to 27°C) provided the display light level is 100 fc (1.1 klux) or higher. Displaying plants in unheated areas where temperatures are below 50°F (10°C), even for brief periods at night, is harmful.

Irrigation. Keep plants uniformly moist at all times, as they are very sensitive to drying out. Flowers and bracts will drop if plants are allowed to wilt slightly.

Disorder. Flower drop: Flower and bract drop can be caused by exposure to ethylene, drying out, extended shipping periods or use of low light (less than 100 fc [1.1 klux]) during the retail display period.

Consumer care

Light. Plants do best under high light conditions. Provide light levels of 100 fc (1.1 klux) or more. Flower and leaf drop will occur on plants placed at light levels of 50 fc (.5 klux) or less.

Temperature. Provide interior temperatures from 60° to 80°F (16° to 24°C).

Location. Choose a south, east or west window that provides high light levels. Bougainvillea can be used successfully as patio plants once flowering has terminated indoors, but avoid temperatures below 50°F (10°C) to eliminate chilling injury.

Irrigation. Proper watering is important. Bracts and leaves will drop if plants dry out, regardless of the interior light and temperature levels. Water plants thoroughly at each irrigation so that the entire root ball is wet.

Grooming. Remove yellow leaves or faded flowers.

Disorder. Flower drop: Flowers drop when plants are exposed to ethylene, placed under low light conditions or allowed to dry out.

Cultivars. A number of cultivars are available, but no information is available on their longevity.

ADDITIONAL READING
Cameron, A.C. and M.S. Reid. 1983. Use of silver thiosulfate to prevent flower abscission from potted plants. *Scientia Horticultura* 19:373-378.
Hackett, W.P. and R.M. Sachs. 1985. Bougainvillea. A.H. Halevy, ed. *Handbook of Flowering, Vol. II.* Boca Raton, FL: CRC Press Inc.

Calceolaria crenatiflora kal-see-oh-*lay*-ree-uh kren-at-i-*flor*-uh

Also: *C. herbeohybrida*
Family Name: **Scrophulariaceae**
Common Names: **Calceolaria, Slipperwort, Slipper Flower, Pocketbook Flower, Pouch Flower**

C

Originated in Mexico, Chile and Argentina—about 500 species of herbaceous and shrubby plants. Probably the parent of cultivars sometimes known collectively as *C. herbeohybrida* (*C. hybrida*). Plants are usually dwarf or small (2 feet [.6 m] or less), bearing flowers with large inflated pouches of many colors.

ANYTIME

Production factors

No information is available on the effects of environmental conditions or cultural factors on calceolaria longevity.

Development stage. Market plants when four to eight flowers are open and remaining buds are visible or showing color.

Problems. Diseases: Stem rot, Botrytis.

Insects: Aphids, spider mites and whitefly.

Disorder. Uneven flowering: This problem is most commonly caused by inadequate cooling prior to forcing.

Postproduction factors

Shipping, handling and storage

Temperature. Ship plants at temperatures ranging from 41° to 60°F (5° to 16°C) without harmful effects, provided shipping duration does not exceed 6 days. Avoid boxing warm plants that have just been watered if cold shipping temperatures (35° to 45°F [2° to 7°C]) are used. In this situation, moisture condenses as the temperature is lowered, collects on the flowers and leaves, and can result in Botrytis. Some cultivars will not be affected, but others are sensitive to Botrytis.

Gases. Exposure to ethylene causes flowers to drop. Application of silver thiosulfate as a 0.5 mM spray reduces, but does not eliminate, flower drop.

Lasting qualities. Plants may last 4 to 5 weeks, depending on interior conditions and cultivar used.

Calceolaria crenatiflora

kal-see-oh-*lay*-ree-uh
kren-at-i-*flor*-uh

C

Care and grooming. Lower leaves may become light green or yellow as plants begin to flower, and Botrytis may be evident on the blooms of some cultivars at flowering. Remove these leaves and flowers before plants are sleeved, boxed and shipped to retail markets.

Retail handling

Light. Display plants at light levels of 50 to 100 fc (.5 to 1.1 klux).

Temperature. Maintain temperatures of 65° to 70°F (18° to 21°C) if possible. Plants will decline rapidly if the sales area is 80°F (27°C) or higher.

Irrigation. Calceolaria require large amounts of water, or they wilt rapidly. However, roots will be damaged and die if plants are overwatered. Don't allow plants to dry out.

Disorder. Flower drop: This problem may be caused by exposure to ethylene or extended periods in the dark.

Consumer care

Light. Keep light levels at 25 to 100 fc (.3 to 1.1 klux) for satisfactory interior performance. New flowers will develop for longer periods of time at higher light levels.

Temperature. Provide cool temperatures of 65° to 75°F (18° to 24°C).

Irrigation. One of the biggest problems with calceolaria is drying out. Keep plants uniformly watered, but not overwatered, at all times.

Grooming. Remove older flowers that turn brown as new flowers develop.

Disorder. Botrytis on the flowers: Flower margins may appear water-soaked and brown. This condition is most common when flowers are moistened repeatedly as plants are watered. Keep water off flowers and foliage.

Cultivars. A number of seed-propagated varieties are available as selections of mixed colors. No specific cultivars or color selections are available. There are differences in interior longevity and Botrytis susceptibility within these mixtures.

ADDITIONAL READING
Cameron, A.C., M.S. Reid and G.W. Hickman. 1981. Using STS to prevent flower shattering in potted flowering plants—progress report. *Flower and Nursery Report: Fall.* Cooperative Extension Bulletin. University of California, Davis, CA.
Kho, Y.O. and J. Baer. 1978. Improvement of flowering in calceolaria by cold treatment and selection. *Neth. J. Agric. Sci.* 26:106-109.

Clerodendrum thomsoniae cler-oh-*den*-drum *tom*-son-ee-ee

Family Name: **Verbenaceae**
Common Names: **Bleeding Glory-Bower, Tropical Bleeding-Heart, Glory Tree, Bag-Flower**

Originated in West Africa—over 450 species of deciduous or evergreen trees or shrubs, sometimes climbing. Native to the tropics, but mostly to the East Hemisphere. These cultivars are grown in greenhouses or outdoors in the southern United States and California.

BLEEDING-HEART VINE

Production factors

Light. Low light during production will increase flower and bud abscission.

Temperature. Avoid high production temperatures to reduce flower and bud abscission.

Development stage. Market plants with approximately 25% of the flowers fully colored and numerous buds present.

Problems. Diseases: Botrytis, tobacco ringspot virus.

Insect: Whitefly.

Disorder. Flower drop: This problem has been related to production under high temperature and low light conditions.

Postproduction factors

Shipping, handling and storage

Light. Avoid storing and shipping periods of longer than 3 days without lights to prevent excessive flower drop.

Temperature. Ship plants at 50° to 55°F (10° to 13°C). Because plants are chilling-sensitive, avoid temperatures below 46°F (8°C) to prevent flower drop. High storage and shipping temperatures (60°F [16°C] or greater) are also harmful.

Gases. Exposure to ethylene will result in flower drop. Increased CO_2 concentration during storage has not been beneficial in reducing flower drop.

Lasting qualities. Plants will flower and continue to develop existing buds for 3 to 4 weeks when properly handled and maintained in the interior.

Care and grooming. Remove damaged leaves and flowers before storage and shipping.

Clerodendrum thomsoniae   cler-oh-*den*-drum *tom*-son-ee-ee

C

Retail handling

Light. Display plants at light levels of 50 to 100 fc (.5 to 1.1 klux) or higher. While higher light levels are desirable, avoid direct sunlight.

Temperature. Display the plants at 60° to 80°F (16° to 27°C). Don't hold plants in areas with night temperatures below 50°F (10°C).

Irrigation. Water plants thoroughly before the soil becomes dry to the touch. Flowers will drop if the plants dry out.

Disorder. Flower drop: A common cause of this problem is exposure to ethylene during shipping, storage or retail display. Other factors, such as drying out and exposure to cold air drafts in the retail sales area, contribute to flower drop.

Consumer care

Light. Clerodendrum do well at light levels of 50 fc (.5 klux) or higher.

Temperature. Maintain temperatures of 65° to 80°F (18° to 27°C), and avoid cold air drafts.

Location. Choose an east, south or west window.

Irrigation. Keep the soil moist at all times; drying out causes flower drop.

Grooming. Remove flowers as the color fades.

ADDITIONAL READING

Adriasen, A.F. 1980. *Transport of opbevaring af Clerodendrum. Gartner Tidende* 96:314-315.

Hammer, P.A. 1980. Other flowering pot plants. R.A. Larson, ed. *Introduction to Floriculture.* New York: Academic Press Inc.

Hildrum, H. 1972. New pot plant—*Clerodendrum thomsoniae* Balf. *N.Y. State Flower Ind. Bull.* Nov./Dec.

Crocus spp.

Family Name: **Iridaceae**
Common Name: **Crocus**

Originated in Spain, North Africa to Afghanistan, and the Mediterranean—about 75 to 80 species of cormous herbs. Plants have linear, grasslike or keeled leaves and tubular formed, six-segmented flowers ranging in colors from white, yellow or lilac to deep purple.

C

CROCUS

Production factors

No information is available on the effects of production light, temperature, media or fertilization on crocus longevity.

Development stage. Market plants at the sprout stage for best performance.

Disorder. Flower abortion: This problem is usually due to forcing cultivars in the wrong flowering period or to insufficient periods of cold treatment.

Postproduction factors

Shipping, handling and storage

Light. Crocus can tolerate shipping in closed containers without light for 3 days.

Temperature. Ship or store plants at 33° to 35°F (0° to 2°C). Avoid shipping and holding periods of more than 3 days to maximize longevity.

Retail handling

Light. Display plants at 50 fc (.5 klux) or higher.

Temperature. Maintain temperatures from 60° to 70°F (16° to 20°C). Plants develop rapidly if displayed at warm temperatures.

Lasting qualities. Crocus will flower 4 to 7 days indoors.

Irrigation. Keep crocus moist at all times during marketing.

Consumer care

Light. Light levels as low as 50 fc (.5 klux) are satisfactory for crocus.

Crocus spp. *kroh*-kus

Temperature. Plants will last 3 to 4 days longer if maintained at 65°F (18°C) compared to 80°F (27°C).

Irrigation. Keep medium uniformly moist, using tepid water at each watering.

Grooming. Remove flower stalks as the flowers become faded.

Cultivars. Cultivars are available in flower colors of lavender, yellow and white, and with striped pattern. Longevity differences between cultivars is unknown.

ADDITIONAL READING

De Hertogh, A.A. 1985. *Holland Bulb Forcers Guide*. New York: Netherlands Flower-Bulb Institute.

Nell, T.A., A.A. De Hertogh and J.E. Barrett. 1991. Bulbs as flowering potted plants—keys to increased longevity. *GrowerTalks* 55(7):57-60.

Crossandra infundibuliformis

kros-*san*-druh in-fun-dih-bull-if-*for*-mis

Also: *C. undulifolia*
Family Name: **Acanthaceae**
Common Names: **Crossandra, Firecracker Flower**

Originated in South India and Ceylon—about 50 species of glabrous or pubescent shrubs or herbs. Crossandra are grown under glass or outdoors in warm countries and the tropics.

CROSSANDRA

Production factors

No information is available on the effects of production temperature, nutrition or media on the interior longevity of crossandra.

Light. Plants grown at low production light levels (300 to 900 fc [3 to 9 klux]) perform best in an interior environment.

Problem. Insect: Aphids.

Postproduction factors

Shipping, handling and storage
   Temperature. Crossandra are sensitive to cold temperatures. Leaves become black on plants held at 40°F (4°C). Store and ship plants at temperatures from 50° to 55°F (10° to 13°C).

   Gases. Exposure to ethylene causes florets to drop. Avoid storage and shipping temperatures above 65°F (18°C) since injury due to ethylene is greater at higher temperatures.

   Lasting qualities. Plants will live 21 to 28 days with proper handling.

   Care and grooming. Remove damaged leaves and flowers before sleeving.

Retail handling

   Light. Maintain plants at light levels of 300 to 1,000 fc [3 to 10 klux] to maximize their lifespan.

   Temperature. Display plants in areas with temperatures higher than 55°F (13°C).

   Irrigation. Water crossandra before the soil becomes dry. Avoid overwatering as it damages the root system.

Disorders. Black leaves: This is caused by exposure to temperatures below 50°F (10°C). Flower drop: This problem results from exposure to ethylene, extended storage and shipping durations or placement in low light conditions.

Consumer care

Light. Plants will continue to flower in the interior with 300 to 1,000 fc [3 to 10 klux] of light. Provide long days to allow additional new flower buds to form at these light levels. Choose an east, south or west window that provides low to medium light to maximize plants' life.

Temperature. Maintain plants at 65° to 80°F (18° to 27°C). Don't expose crossandra to temperatures below 50°F (10°C).

Irrigation. Keep crossandra uniformly moist. Don't overwater or plant roots will die.

Grooming. Remove individual flowers as needed to maintain an attractive plant.

Disorders. Failure of plant to flower: This problem is caused by maintaining plant under short-day conditions.

Cultivars. The most common cultivar is Mona Wallhed. Other cultivars are available with red, bright orange, yellow, salmon pink or pink flowers. Information is not available on the postproduction characteristics of these cultivars.

ADDITIONAL READING

Krazewski, R.A. and D.P. Ormrod. 1986. Utilization of a response surface technique to study light acclimation of indoor flowering plants. *Journal of the American Society of Horticultural Science* 111:47-55.

Wilkins, H.F. 1985. *Crossandra infundibuliformis.* A.H. Halevy, ed. *The Handbook of Flowering.* Boca Raton, FL: CRC Presses Inc.

Cyclamen persicum

sye-kluh-men
per-sih-kum

Family Name: **Primulaceae**
Common Names: **Cyclamen, Florist's Cyclamen**

Originated in Central Europe and the Mediterranean to Iran—15 species of tuberous herbs. *C. persicum* is a popular florist's plant. Others are grown outdoors if climate permits, and tender ones are grown in pots.

SIERRA LILAC

Production factors

No information is available on the effects of production light level, nutrition or media on cyclamen longevity.

Temperature. Longevity was increased at production temperatures of 62°F (17°C) compared to 55°F (13°C) for Rose of Aalsmeer, White Caramel Eye, Cattleya, Rose of Marienthal and Pearl of Zehlendorf. Growing these cultivars at 62°F (17°C) also reduced the time from seeding to flowering.

Results differ between cultivars.

Development stage. Market plants when there are two to three open flowers and numerous buds are showing color. Because buds will open indoors with proper care, only those that show the flower color to the customer are necessary for marketing.

Problems. Diseases: Botrytis, crown rot, root rot, basal stem rot, black root rot, brown root rot, gray mold and stunt.

Insects: Cyclamen mites, spider mites, aphids, thrips and fungus gnats.

Disorders. Bud drop: This problem may be caused by high temperatures, low production light levels, drying out or high fertilizer levels.

Tall plants and weak growth: These may be a result of close spacing, high production temperatures, low production light levels or high nutrition levels.

Small flowers: High temperatures and overfertilization are the primary causes.

Postproduction factors

Shipping, handling and storage

Light. Cyclamen will tolerate 3 to 6 days of shipping in closed boxes at proper temperatures without harmful effects. Longer periods lead to diseased foliage and wilting of the flower stalks.

Cyclamen persicum

sye-kluh-men
per-sih-kum

Temperature. Ship and store cyclamen from 41°F (5°C) to 50°F (10°C). Shipping duration should not exceed 7 days. Avoid packing plants in warm areas before transport as Botrytis may become a problem if plants are shipped at low temperatures.

Gases. Flower wilt and drop will occur if plants are exposed to ethylene. No work has been published on the effects of silver thiosulfate in minimizing ethylene effects.

Lasting qualities. Flowers will last 3 to 4 weeks in the interior if maintained properly.

Care and grooming. Remove faded flowers and yellow leaves daily to assure continuous blooming.

Retail handling

Light. Display plants at high light (100 fc [1.1 klux] or greater). Avoid direct sunlight. Leaf yellowing and rapid flower decline may occur at light levels of 25 fc (270 lux) or lower.

Temperature. Provide cool temperatures, preferably from 60° to 68°F (16° to 20°C). Display temperatures can drop to 50°F (10°C) without damage.

Irrigation. Keep medium moist at all times. Don't allow plants to wilt, or flower longevity will decrease and yellowing of leaves will increase.

Disorder. Bud drop: High temperatures, low light, drying out, high production fertilizer levels and exposure to ethylene will promote bud drop.

Consumer care

Light. Provide minimum light level of 100 fc (1.1 klux) for development of the largest numbers of flower buds. Light levels of 25 fc (270 lux) or lower cause leaves to become yellow and flower stalks to elongate.

Temperature. Keep plants at cool temperatures from 58° to 68°F (15 to 20°C). Research has shown that longevity is greatest at cool interior temperatures (62°F, 17°C) compared to temperatures of 66°F, 72°F and 77°F (19°C, 22°C and 25°C). Rapid flower and plant decline occurs, and flowering ceases at higher temperatures.

Location. Place plants near any window location.

Irrigation. Keep cyclamen moist at all times, and don't allow them to dry out. Avoid getting water on the crown of the plants.

Grooming. Remove faded flowers and yellow leaves.

Disorder. Bud drop: This is caused by placing plants in areas of high temperatures or low light, or allowing plants to dry out.

Cultivars. Numerous standard (for large containers) and miniature flowering (for 2- to 4-inch [5- to 10-cm] containers) cyclamen varieties are now available from seed suppliers. New introductions offer predictability in flowering time, free flowering habit and excellent plant form. Flower colors include red, pink, salmon, scarlet, white and various shades of these colors. Seeds are available in single-color selections and as color mixtures. Longevity does vary between cultivars, but evaluations have not been conducted with many of those currently on the market.

ADDITIONAL READING
Molinar, J.M. and C.J. Williams. 1977. Response of *cyclamen persicum* cultivars to different growing and holding temperatures. *Can. J. Plant Sci.* 57:93-100.
Sterling, E.P. and W.H. Molenaar. 1985. *Transport tolerantie van potplanten. Mededeling Nr. 39..* Wageningen, The Netherlands: Sprenger Institute.

C

Dendranthema grandiflora

den-*dran*-the-ma
gran-di-*flor*-ruh

Family Name: **Compositae**
Common Names: **Florist's Chrysanthemum, Mum**

Formerly classified as *Chrysanthemum* **x** *morifolium*. Originated in Japan—grown primarily as ornamental plants. Assumed to be a hybrid involving *Chrysanthemum indicum*, *C. japonense* (Mak.) Nakai, *C. makinoi*, *C. ornatum* Hemsl and perhaps even other species. Cultivated chrysanthemums are hardy or half-hardy, mostly aromatic, coarse plants, with flowers in a wide range of colors; they usually bloom late in the autumn in the open. They may be flowering pot plants or cut flowers year-round, chiefly through control of day length.

D

SUNNY MANDALAY

Production factors

Ease of production, crop predictability and good interior performance are among the factors that have made chrysanthemum the major year-round flowering pot plant.

Light. Produce plants at recommended light levels of 5,000 to 6,000 fc (53.8 to 64.6 klux) to maximize their longevity. In Northern production areas, supplemental high intensity lighting may increase the longevity during the low-light winter months. Shading may be required during the final 1 to 2 weeks during high light periods of production to avoid sunscald on the flowers, especially on white cultivars.

Temperature. Low night temperatures of 58°F to 60°F (14° to 16°C) during the final 4 weeks of production will intensify flower color. These low temperatures may lead to pinking on some white cultivars. High night temperatures of 65° to 75°F (18° to 24°C) don't reduce longevity.

Nutrition. High fertilizer levels decrease longevity. Plants fertilized with 150 ppm nitrogen at every irrigation lasted 7 to 14 days longer than plants fertilized with 450 ppm nitrogen, depending on the cultivar and growing medium. Complete termination of fertilizer at disbud extends the longevity 7 to 10 days without any harmful effects like reduced leaf color or flower size. The specific increase in longevity that results from fertilizer termination is related to the fertilization level during production and the cultivar being grown.

Use a fertilization program that provides

D

60% to 70% of the nitrogen in a nitrate form and the remainder from ammonia and urea sources. Also use a nitrogen:potassium ratio of 1:1 throughout the crop. No benefit has been observed from changing the nitrogen:potassium ratio during the final weeks of the crop cycle.

Irrigation. Keep plants uniformly moist during production and avoid wilting. Withholding water during flower development reduces flower size, delays flowering and possibly injures leaves without an increase in longevity. Overwatering may damage roots and reduce longevity.

Media. Use soil and soilless media with good aeration and drainage to produce high-quality plants. The addition of 20% soil to soilless media has been shown to increase longevity; however, many of the soilless media offer good production and postproduction characteristics.

Development stage. Market plants when flowers are 50% open. Immature flowers (50% or less open) will be reduced in size and have decreased flower color intensity as they develop under interior conditions.

Problems. Diseases: Ascochyta blight, Botrytis, Fusarium, powdery mildew, Pythium, Rhizoctonia, rust, Sclerotinia sclerotiorum, septoria leaf spot, stunt, Verticillium wilt and yellows.

Insects: Aphids, cutworms, foliar and root knot nematodes, grasshoppers, leaf miners, leaf rollers, loopers, mealybugs, chrysanthemum midges, slugs, sowbugs, spider mites, spittle bugs, symphylids, tarnished plant bugs, termites and thrips.

Shipping, handling and storage

Light. Most varieties may be stored in the dark for 7 days at 35° to 40°F (2° to 4°C) without a loss of quality or longevity if fertilization is ended at disbud.

Temperature. Store and ship plants at 35° to 40°F (2° to 4°C) to maximize longevity. Hydrocooling, precooling and forced air cooling may be used, but increases in longevity have not been demonstrated with these procedures.

Gases. Chrysanthemums are one of very few flowering crops that experience virtually no negative effects from ethylene exposure. One study, however, has reported increased growth of flower mold in chrysanthemums following exposure to ethylene.

Care and grooming. Remove damaged foliage and flowers before shipping. If the diseased plant parts can't be removed, discard the plants.

Retail handling

Light. Keep light levels in the display area at 50 fc (.5 klux) or greater. Because of their tolerance to ethylene, chrysanthemums are ideal for retail sales in supermarkets and many other settings, as long as direct sunlight is avoided.

Temperature. Maintain display temperatures at 65° to 75°F (18° to 24°C).

Irrigation. Keep growing medium uniformly moist. Overwatering or allowing plants to wilt damages the root system and decreases longevity. Applying film-forming antitranspirants will reduce water loss approximately 20%, but this has not been shown to increase longevity.

Dendranthema grandiflora

den-*dran*-the-ma
gran-di-*flor*-ruh

Disorders. Yellow leaves: This may be caused by overwatering, underwatering, high shipping temperatures, high production fertilizer levels and the cultivar itself.

Flower fading: Marketing plants at an immature stage or maintaining high production temperatures or low light levels in the display area contribute to fading.

Consumer care

Light. Provide natural and artificial light levels of 50 fc (.5 klux) for 8 to 10 hours daily.

Temperature. Provide temperatures of 65° to 70°F (18 to 21°C) for optimal indoor performance. Higher temperatures will be tolerated, but longevity will decrease.

Location. Place plants in areas providing good light levels, but avoid direct light and air drafts.

D

Chrysanthemum Cultivars Offering Longevity

Color	Very good longevity	Excellent longevity	Color	Very good longevity	Excellent longevity
White	Boald	Envy	Pink	Blush	
	Claro	Winter Carnival		Capri	
	Dana			Charm	
	Dare			Chic	
	Free Spirit			Circus	
	Karma			Coral Charm	
	Kiss			Dark Circus	
	Mountain Snow			Dark Pomona	
	Paragon			Deep Luv	
	Puritan			Engarde	
	Raya			Loyalty	
	Solo			Luv	
	Spirit			Pasadena	
	Surf			Pomona	
	Windsong			Royal Trophy	
Yellow	Bright Golden Anne	Iridon		Skylight	
	Carnival	Vista		Splendor	
	Cartago	Yellow Envy		Tasca	
	Cream Boaldi			Tempo	
	Dark Yellow Paragon			Twilight	
	Eureka		Bronze	Cherry Pomona	Redding
	Gold Champ			Cirbronze	Salmon Splendor
	Hopscotch			Dark Bronze Charm	
	Indio			Favor	
	Miramar			Glowing Mandalay	
	Mountain Peak			Lucido	
	Pico			Mandarin Red Torch	
	Songster			Salmon Charm	
	Spice			Sequest	
	Sunburst Spirit			Stoplight	
	Sunny Mandalay			Theme	
	Surfine			Torch	
	Yellow Boaldi				
	Yellow Favor				
	Yellow Ovaro				
	Yellow Tan				
	Yellow Torch				

Flowering Potted Plants *Dendranthema*

Irrigation. Keep soil uniformly moist. Don't allow plants to wilt repeatedly, or their lifespan will be reduced.

Grooming. Remove yellow leaves and dead flowers.

Cultivars. A wide range of chrysanthemum cultivars offers consumers a selection of vivid colors and diverse flower forms unequaled by any other crop. Some cultivars have exhibited exceptional longevity even under adverse interior conditions.

ADDITIONAL READING

Boodley, J.W., J. Kumpf and B. Pollinger. 1983. An evaluation of soil vs. peat-lite media on postproduction life of selected potted chrysanthemums. *Connecticut Greenhouse Newsletter* 117:11-12.

Davies, J.N. and A.C. Bunt. 1978. Quality in the pot chrysanthemum. *Glass Crops Res. Inst. A.R.* 1978:74-75.

Eikhof, R.H., P.A. King and G.H. Koven. 1974. Control of wilting in potted plants. *Ohio Florists' Association Bulletin* 532:6-7.

Marousky, F.J. 1977. Commodity requirements and recommendations for flowers and nursery stocks. *Contr. Atm. for the Storage and Transp. of Perishable Agr. Commodities.* Second Nat. Contr. Atm. Res. Conf., Mich. St. Univ. 28:287-291.

Martin, J.D. and C.B. Link. 1973. Reducing water loss of potted chrysanthemums with presale application of antitranspirants. *Journal of the American Society of Horticultural Science* 98(3):303-306.

Nell, T.A., M.T. Leonard and J.E. Barrett. 1989. Fertilization termination influences postharvest performance of pot chrysanthemum. *HortScience* 24:996-998.

———. 1990. Production and postproduction irradiance affects acclimatization and longevity of potted chrysanthemum and poinsettia. *Journal of the American Society of Horticultural Science* 115:262-265.

Nell, T.A. 1991. How to make long-lasting, top performers out of your pot mums. *GrowerTalks* 54(10):53-59.

Roude, N. 1988. "Effects of N, K and $NH_4:NO_3$ ratio on growth and longevity of Iridon *Chrysanthemum morifolium*." M.S. thesis, University of Florida.

Roude, N., T.A. Nell and J.E. Barrett. 1990. Nitrogen source and concentration, growing medium, and cultivar affect longevity of potted chrysanthemums. *HortScience* 26:49-52.

———. 1991. Longevity of potted chrysanthemums at various nitrogen and potassium concentrations and $NH_4:NO_4$ ratios. *HortScience* 26:163-165.

Shanks, J.B. 1960. Selection and care of pot plants. *The Maryland Florist* 74:6-21.

Sidles, C.J. 1983. Chrysanthemum: care tips for the florist. What to tell your customers. *Flowers &* 4(10):69-70.

Staby, G.L., J.L. Robertson, D.C. Kiplinger and C.A. Conover. 1976. Chain of life. *Proceedings of the National Floricultural Conference on Commodity Handling.* Hort. Ser. Oh. Ag. Res. Dev. Ctr. 432:71.

Staby, G.L., J.F. Thompson, A.M. Kofranek and V.R. Walter. 1981. Cooling of potted chrysanthemums. *HortScience* 16:566-568.

Sterling, E.P. and W.H. Molenaar. 1985. *Transport tolerantie van potplanten. Mededeling Nr. 39.* Wageningen, The Netherlands: Sprenger Institute.

Walter, V.R. 1972. "Studies on the keeping quality of potted chrysanthemums as affected by differential degree of flower development." M.S. thesis, Ohio State University.

Wesenberg, B.G. and G.E. Beck. 1964. Influence of production environment and other factors on the longevity of potted chrysanthemum flowers (*Chrysanthemum morifolium* Ramat.) *Proceedings of the American Society of Horticultural Science* 85:584-590.

Williams, W.B. and C.O. Box. 1959. Mature flowers better buy in chrysanthemums. *Mississippi Farm Res.* 22(11):7.

Euphorbia pulcherrima

yew-*for*-bee-uh
pull-*kare*-rih-muh

Family Name: **Euphorbiaceae**
Common Names: **Poinsettia, Christmas Star, Christmas Flower, Painted Leaf, Lobster Plant, Mexican Flameleaf**

Mexico—winter-flowering shrub to 10 feet. Many cultivars have been developed, with larger white, pink or various shades of red and bicolor bracts.

ECKESPOINT CELEBRATE

Production factors

Light. Lower production light level to 2,500 fc (26.9 klux) on November 15 to reduce leaf drop in interior conditions. Light levels below 2,500 fc may cause premature cyathia drop.

Temperature. Lower night temperature to 58° to 60°F (14° to 16°C) on November 15 to 20 to enhance bract color and reduce leaf abscission after plants are moved to interior conditions.

Nutrition. Apply low nitrogen rates (3 g of Osmocote or 250 to 300 ppm nitrogen from a 20N-10P-20K soluble fertilizer of a liquid nitrogen, phosphorus and potassium composition fertilizer) to reduce leaf drop. Use of 90- to 100-day slow-release fertilizers is recommended. Avoid multiple applications of Osmocote and fertilizers containing more than 60% ammoniacal nitrogen to reduce bract necrosis and leaf drop. Don't apply fertilizer during the 2 weeks prior to marketing to reduce the chance of leaf drop.

Irrigation. Monitor irrigation frequency carefully to develop a good root system. No benefits have been demonstrated from toning plants by allowing them to wilt before marketing. Leaf and cyathia drop may become a problem if plants are allowed to wilt.

Media. Use a well-drained, porous medium to produce a high-quality plant. No information relating the medium to longevity is available.

Development stage. Market plants when bracts are fully colored and pollen is beginning to show in the cyathia.

Problems. Diseases: Botrytis, Phytophthora, Pythium, Rhizoctonia, scab, Thielaviopsis, Rhizopus, bacterial canker, bacterial leaf spot, bacterial stem rot, greasy canker and crown gall.

Insects: Two-spotted spider mites, scale, fungus gnats, whitefly, beet armyworms, poinsettia hornworms and mealybugs.

Disorders. Bract edge burn: Bract margins become brown and necrotic areas may spread to the center of the bract. Necrosis is most common on Gutbier V-14 Glory, but may occur on other cultivars. The following steps are recommended to minimize bract necrosis:

(1) Avoid high fertilizer rates and heavy watering during the final 4 weeks of production.

(2) Don't use fertilizers with more than 40% of the nitrogen in the ammonia or urea forms.

(3) High rates of Osmocote 14-14-14 should not be used. Limit applications to a single one at planting.

(4) Reduce greenhouse humidity during the final 3 weeks of production.

Premature cyathia bud drop: Bud drop during the final 1 to 3 weeks of production may be caused by production under low light conditions, high production temperatures or crowding plants during production.

Postproduction factors

Shipping, handling and storage

Place plants in paper or plastic sleeves to avoid injury to leaves and bracts during handling and shipping. For the longest lifespan, keep plants sleeved and boxed for the shortest possible time, preferably 3 days or less. The following factors will reduce quality and longevity regardless of shipping time.

Light. Keep the shipping and holding times as short as possible since extended exposure to dark conditions causes premature leaf and cyathia drop.

Temperature. Ship and store plants at 55° to 60°F (13° to 16°C). Temperatures below 50°F (10°C) cause bracts to become white from chilling injury. Higher shipping and/or holding temperatures may lead to fading of bract color, leaf and cyathia drop and reduced longevity. Hold plants at 55° to 60°F (13° to 16°C) once they are sleeved.

Gases. Poinsettias produce ethylene because of the mechanical bending of the leaf petioles during sleeving, regardless of the type of sleeve. Ethylene causes leaves and bracts to droop after the sleeves are removed. Generally, the longer poinsettias are sleeved, the longer it will take for them to recover.

Sensitivity of Cultivars to Ethylene

Susceptible to epinasty	Resistant to epinasty
Annette Hegg Dark Red	Eckespoint C-1 Red
Annette Hegg Diva Starlight	Gutbier V-14 Glory
Annette Hegg Pink	Gutbier V-14 Pink
Annette Hegg Topwhite	Gutbier V-14 Marble
Annette Hegg Lady	Gutbier V-10 Amy
Annette Hegg Marble	Gutbier V-17 Angelika
Peace Cheers! (H-365)	Gutbier V-10 Marble
Peace Regal Velvet	Eckespoint Celebrate
Peace Noel Blush	Eckespoint Freedom
Peace Noel Hot Pink	Eckespoint Jingle Bells 3
Peace Frost	Eckespoint Lilo
Peace Noel	Gross Subjibi

Care and grooming. Remove all injured or diseased leaves and bracts before sleeving.

Retail handling

Plants must be unboxed and unsleeved immediately upon arrival at the retail store.

Light. Place plants in a lighted display area providing 100 fc (1.1 klux) of light from incandescent bulbs or natural light. If fluorescent lighting is used, install cool white fluorescent tubes to provide a true representation of bract color.

Temperature. Keep plants at 65° to 75°F (18° to 24°C).

Irrigation. Water poinsettias only as needed. They may not require water when removed from the box, but soil moisture should be checked daily. Drying out and overwatering cause leaf drop.

Lasting qualities. Poinsettias will last 30 days or longer.

Disorders. Epinasty: Petioles, leaves and bracts droop after plants have been sleeved. The symptoms are worse if plants have been sleeved for long periods or stored at temperatures above 65°F (18°C). Poinsettias will recover within 24 hours if they are unboxed, removed from the sleeves and placed in a well-lighted room maintained at 65°F (18°C). Plants may not recover if they are sleeved too long.

Bract discoloration: Bracts will have a blue tint at storage temperatures of 40° to 45°F (4° to 7°C) or may turn white at temperatures below 40°F (4°C). These bracts will not regain normal color. Displaying plants at light intensities less than 50 fc (.5 klux) or placing them in the interior before bracts are fully colored will lead to bract fading.

Flower drop: The premature drop of flowers and buds is influenced by production conditions, including drying out, low light, high temperature, low humidity or placement near an air conditioner, heater vents or open doors.

Consumer care

Light. Provide good light to maintain good bract color and avoid leaf drop. A minimum of 100 fc (1.1 klux) of light, preferably from incandescent bulbs or cool white fluorescent bulbs, gives good results indoors. Avoid direct sunlight.

Temperature. Maintain plants at 65° to 75°F (18° to 24°C). Temperatures above 75°F (24°C) increase leaf drop, especially when combined with low light conditions. Avoid temperatures below 50°F (10°C) when moving plants to the home or interiorscape.

Location. Place poinsettias in a well-lighted area without exposure to cold air drafts.

Irrigation. Keep plants moist at all times as drying out increases leaf drop. Don't use fertilizer unless the plant is kept for more than 30 days.

Grooming. Remove dead and yellow leaves.

Disorders. Leaf drop: This is a natural process that can be affected by drying out, overwatering, placement in a dark location and aging.

Cyathia drop: This disorder is common once plants are moved to low light and low humidity conditions in the interior. Placing plants in a higher light area reduces cyathia drop. Poinsettia cultivars vary in the amount of cyathia abscission once plants are moved indoors.

Regrowth: Move the plant outdoors after the last chance of frost, and trim each stem 3 to 4 inches (7 to 10 cm). Prune the stems again in August, and provide water and fertilizer. The plants must receive short days beginning in late September and continuing until flowering for the holidays.

E

Cultivars. Poinsettia cultivars vary in interior longevity. The Hegg group, Gutbier V-14 Glory and Eckespoint Freedom plants do well under interior conditions. Eckespoint Lilo is excellent indoors. Several new cultivars have been introduced in the last 2 to 3 years, but in-depth interior performance evaluations have not been completed at this time. A summary of the handling and longevity of some cultivars is presented below.

E

Postharvest Performance of Some Cultivars

Variety name	Keeping quality	Shipping and handling quality	Susceptible to epinasty
Eckespoint Lilo	Excellent. Longest lasting variety.	Excellent. Recovers rapidly shipping.	No
Eckespoint Celebrate	Very good.	Ships very well.	No
Gutbier V-14 Glory	Very good.	Ships well. Sensitive to bruising.	No
Eckespoint Freedom	Very good.	Ships well.	No
Annette Hegg	Excellent. Very long lasting.	Ships well.	Yes

ADDITIONAL READING

Bush, P. 1982. Poinsettias: Ecke echoes grower concerns of mass-market care, handling. *Produce & Floral Retailing* 89:16-17.

Carpenter, W.J. 1956. The influence of plant hormones on the abscission of poinsettia leaves and bracts. *Proceedings of the American Society of Horticultural Science* 67:539-544.

Corr, B. and B.A. Eisenberg. 1982. Improving the postharvest handling of holiday flowering plants. *Ill. St. Flor. Assoc. Bul.* 405:7-9.

Eskilson, M.D. 1984. Poinsettia: care tips for florist and consumer. *Flowers &* 5:65.

Marousky, F.J. and J.B. Shanks. 1966. Effects of environmental factors and plant maturity as bract and leaf abscission in *Euphorbia pulcherrima* Willd. *Proceedings of the American Society of Horticultural Science* 88:662-670.

Mehte, R.D. 1979. Effect of two hydrophilic polymers on keeping quality, growth, and development of poinsettias grown in two media. *HortScience* 14:432-433.

Miller, S. and R.D. Heins. 1983. Variation in cyathia abscission of poinsettia cultivars in a greenhouse and a simulated postharvest environment. *HortScience* 21:270-272.

Nell, T.A. 1989. The right variety adds more to your bottom line. *GrowerTalks* 52(9):48-50, 52, 54-55.

Nell, T.A. and J.E. Barrett. 1986. Growth and incidence of bract necrosis in Gutbier V-14 Glory poinsettia. *Journal of the American Society of Horticultural Science* 111:266-269.

———. 1986. Influence of simulated shipping on the interior performance of poinsettias. *HortScience* 21:310-312.

E

————. 1986. Production light level effects on light compensation point, carbon exchange rate and postproduction longevity of poinsettias. *Acta Horticultura* 181:257-262.

————. 1991. Plan now to eliminate bract edge burn in your '91 poinsettias. *GrowerTalks* 54(11):18-19.

Nell, T.A., R.T. Leonard and J.E. Barrett. 1990. Production and postproduction irradiance affects acclimatization and longevity of potted chrysanthemum and poinsettia. *Journal of the American Society of Horticultural Science* 115:262-265.

Reid, M.S., Y. Mor and A.M. Kofranek. 1981. Epinasty of poinsettias to the role of auxin and ethylene. *Plant Physiol.* 67:950-952.

Saltveit, M.E. and R.A. Larson. 1981. Reducing leaf epinasty in mechanically stressed poinsettia plants. *Journal of the American Society of Horticultural Science* 106:156-159.

————. 1983. Effect of mechanical stress and inhibitors of protein synthesis on leaf epinasty in mechanically stressed poinsettia plants. *Journal of the American Society of Horticultural Science* 108:253-257.

Saltveit, M.E., D.M. Pharr and R.A. Larson. 1979. Mechanical stress induces ethylene production and epinasty in poinsettia cultivars. *HortScience* 104:452-455.

Scott, L.F. and T.M. Blessington. 1981. Influence of micronutrient sources, dark storage and artificial light on growth and interior quality of *Poinsettia pulcherrima* cultivars. *HortScience* 16:416.

Scott, L.F., T.M. Blessington and J.A. Price. 1982. Postharvest performance of poinsettia as affected by micronutrient source, storage and cultivar. *HortScience* 17:901-902.

————. 1983. Postharvest effects of temperature, dark storage duration, and sleeving on quality retention of Gutbier V-14 Glory poinsettia. *HortScience* 18:749-750.

————. 1984. Postharvest effects of storage method and duration on quality retention of poinsettias. *HortScience* 19:290-291.

————. 1984. Influence of controlled-release fertilizers, storage duration, and light source on postharvest quality of poinsettia. *HortScience* 19:111-112.

Shanks, J.B. 1961. Temperature, maturity, and the keeping of poinsettias under home conditions. *Maryland Florist* 78:4-6.

Staby, G.L., J.F. Thompson and A.M. Kofranek. 1978. Postharvest characteristics of poinsettias as influenced by handling and storage procedures. *Journal of the American Society of Horticultural Science* 103:712-715.

Staby, G.L. and A.M. Kofranek. 1979. Production conditions as they affect harvest and postharvest characteristics of poinsettias. *Journal of the American Society of Horticultural Science* 104:88-92.

Staby, G.L., B.A. Eisenberg, J.W. Kelly, M.P. Bridgen and M.S. Cunningham. 1980. Leaf petiole epinasty in poinsettias. *HortScience* 15:635-636.

Sterling, E.P. and W.H. Molenaar. 1985. *Transport tolerantie van potplanten. Mededeling Nr. 39.* Wageningen, The Netherlands: Sprenger Institute.

Exacum affine

ex-uh-kum
ah-*fin*-ee

Family Name: **Gentianaceae**
Common Names: **Persian Violet, German Violet**

Socotra—about 20 to 30 species of Old World herbs. The annual or biannual plants are grown under glass or outdoors in warm regions.

BEST BLUE

Production factors

No information is available on the effects of production light level, temperature or media on exacum longevity.

Nutrition. The lifespan of exacum decreases with high fertilization rates (5 or 7 kg/m³) provided from Osmocote 18-6-12 or 14-14-14. High rates of liquid fertilizer may also decrease longevity.

Development stage. Market the plants when 10% to 20% of the flowers are open.

The remaining buds will open indoors under the conditions described below.

Problems. Diseases: Botrytis, Pythium and Phytophthora.

Insects: Broad mites, caterpillars, whitefly, thrips and mealybugs.

Disorder. Failure of flowers to open: Blooms on the double-flowered cultivars frequently fail to open once they have reached flower color, a problem that appears to be inherent in these cultivars. Gibberellic acid application has been reported to minimize this problem; however, many commercial growers haven't achieved good results with this procedure.

Postproduction factors

Shipping, handling and storage

Temperature. Exacum are sensitive to cold temperatures. Plants stored at 40°F (4°C) develop black spots on the foliage, making them unmarketable. Ship plants at 55° to 60°F (13° to 16°C).

Lasting qualities. Exacum continue to flower in the interior for 3 to 4 weeks or longer.

Care and grooming. Remove any damaged leaves and flowers before plants are sleeved and stored or shipped.

Exacum affine

ex-uh-kum
ah-*fin*-ee

Retail handling

Light. Display plants in an area with 50 to 100 fc (.5 to 1.1 klux) of light.

Temperature. Maintain temperatures of 65° to 80°F (18° to 27°C).

Irrigation. Water plants when soil becomes dry to the touch. Overwatering can cause root problems.

Disorder. Black spots on the foliage: This is caused by plants being stored or shipped at temperatures below 50°F (10°C).

Consumer care

Light. Provide light levels of 50 to 100 fc (.5 to 1.1 klux) for acceptable plant quality and bud opening. Plants will do well at higher light levels, but avoid full sun since leaf and flower scald may occur.

Temperature. Don't expose exacum to cold drafts. Maintain plants at temperatures from 65° to 80°F (18° to 27°C) for best interior performance. Information is not available on the maximum shipping duration that these plants will tolerate.

Irrigation. Keep plants moist at all times but don't overwater. Water only as soil becomes dry to the touch. The flowers will die if plants are allowed to wilt.

Grooming. Remove individual flowers as they die to promote opening of the remaining buds and continued flowering.

Disorder. Flower fading: This is caused by keeping the plants in low-light, warm-temperature conditions for extended periods.

Cultivars. Blue- and white-petaled cultivars are available. No longevity information is available on these cultivars.

E

ADDITIONAL READING
Furry, M.Z. and M.L. Albrecht. 1986. Exacum, an overlooked florist crop. *Kansas Flora* 4(3):1-2.
Harbaugh, B.K. and W.E. Waters. 1982. Influence of controlled-release fertilizer on *Exacum affine* Balf. F. Elfin during production and subsequent simulated home conditions. *HortScience* 17:605-606.
Larson, R.A. 1981. Commercial production of exacum. *North Carolina Flower Growers Bulletin* 25(4):1-6.

45

Flowering Potted Plants *Exacum*

Freesia alba

free-shuh al-ba

Also: *Freesia* x *hybrida* **L.H. Bailey,** *Freesia refracta* **(Jacq.) Klatt**
Family Name: **Iridaceae**
Common Name: **Freesia**

South Africa—about 19 species of cormous herbs. These plants have a tunicate corm with few 2-ranked linear leaves. The inflorescence is in a spike form, the perianth is in a funnel form, and the fragrant flowers have six segments.

AMADEUS

Production factors

No information is available on the effects of production light, temperature, media or fertilizer on freesia longevity.

Development stage. For optimum flowering, market plants when the first floret on each inflorescence begins to open.

Disorders. Flower abortion: This problem is usually due to low forcing light intensity and/ or high forcing temperature during the period of rapid flower development.

Leaf scorch: This problem is caused by the presence of fluoride. Avoid superphosphate or other amendments that contain fluoride.

Postproduction factors

Shipping, handling and storage

Light. Shipping for 3 to 4 days at recommended temperatures will not reduce longevity.

Temperature. Ship or store plants at 33° to 35°F (0.5° to 2°C) for a short duration. High shipping temperatures will cause leaf yellowing once plants are indoors.

Gases. Freesia are sensitive to ethylene, so avoid exposure during shipping and display. Applying silver thiosulfate can be beneficial in some instances.

Irrigation. Keep plants moist during shipping. Avoid watering at time of boxing,

F

Freesia alba

free-shuh *al*-ba

or flower and foliage disease problems may occur because of high humidity levels in the box.

Lasting qualities. Plants will last 10 to 17 days.

Retail handling

Light. Plants will tolerate display light levels as low as 50 fc (.5 klux). Higher light levels may be beneficial if the proper temperatures are maintained and plants are not allowed to dry out.

Temperature. Display plants at 60° to 70°F (16° to 20°C). Display temperatures as low as 50°F (10°C) can be used. Avoid display temperatures above 75°F (24°C) because freesia are sensitive to high temperatures and may develop yellow leaves.

Irrigation. Keep freesia moist at all times. Drying out and overwatering cause leaf yellowing and reduced longevity.

Consumer care

Light. Place plants at light levels of 50 to 100 fc (.5 to 1.1 klux) for good results.

Temperature. Freesia lifespan can be extended by 8 to 10 days by maintaining the plants at 65°F (18°C) compared to 80°F (27°C). Leaf yellowing and rapid flower decline occur at high temperatures.

Irrigation. Keep growing medium uniformly moist at all times.

Grooming. Remove individual flowers as they lose quality.

Cultivars. Freesia cultivars are available in many flower colors. Longevity differences between these cultivars is unknown.

ADDITIONAL READING

De Hertogh, A.A. 1985. *Holland Bulb Forcers Guide*. New York: Netherlands Flower Bulb Institute.

Spikman, G. 1987. Ethylene production, ACC and MACC content of freesia buds and florets. *Scientia Horticultura* 33:291-297.

———. 1989. Development and ethylene production of buds and florets of cut freesia inflorescences as influenced by silver thiosulfate, aminoethoxyvinylglycine and sucrose. *Scientia Horticultura* 39:73-81.

F

Hibiscus rosa-sinensis

hye-*biss*-kus
roh-zuh-sye-*nen*-siss

Family Name: **Malvaceae**
Common Names: **Chinese Hibiscus, Hawaiian Hibiscus, Rose-of-China, China Rose, Blacking Plant**

Asia—about 250 species of herbs, shrubs and trees in warm temperature and tropical regions. Hibiscus are grown as ornamentals in North America. The named cultivars of *H. rosa-sinensis* are propagated by cuttings, grafting or layering.

H

BRILLIANT

Production factors

No information is available on the effects of cultural and environmental production conditions on interior hibiscus longevity.

Development stage. Market plants when two to three flowers are open and other buds are showing color. Numerous small buds should also be present.

Problems. Disease: Botrytis.
Insects: Aphids, red spiders and whitefly.

Disorder. Bud drop: This problem may be caused by drying out, low light conditions or insect and disease problems during production.

Postproduction factors

Shipping, handling and storage

Sleeve and store plants for only short periods. Holding or shipping for longer than 4 days or shorter periods at nonrecommended temperatures causes leaf yellowing and excessive bud drop.

Light. Plants are usually shipped in a closed, dark box. The absence of light is not a problem if shipping and holding time doesn't exceed 4 days at recommended temperatures. A cool, well-lighted room is best for plant storage to prevent leaf yellowing and bud drop.

Temperature. Hibiscus are tropical plants that are very sensitive to temperatures below 50°F (10°C). Shipping temperatures of 53° to 55°F (12° to 13°C) are ideal. Higher temperatures during holding or shipping lead to bud drop and possible leaf yellowing.

Gases. Avoid exposing plants to ethylene or buds will drop. Application of silver

Hibiscus rosa-sinensis

thiosulfate reduces bud drop, but results have been so variable that commercial application must be carefully evaluated before use.

Lasting qualities. Each flower generally lasts only 1 day, but a plant maintained under high light conditions will have open flowers for 2 to 3 weeks or longer.

Care and grooming. Remove any damaged or diseased buds and leaves before the plants are sleeved and boxed.

Disorders. Leaf yellowing: Storing or shipping plants in the dark at high temperatures causes this problem.

Bud drop: This problem is caused by exposure to ethylene during shipping or extended periods in the dark. Bud drop is greatest in plants shipped at low (40°F; 4°C) or high (80°F; 27°C) temperatures for 4 days or longer. Shorter shipping periods may also be harmful, depending on variety and temperature and ethylene concentration.

Retail handling

Light. Display plants at light levels of 100 fc (1.1 klux) or higher to minimize bud drop.

Temperature. Keep temperatures at 65° to 80°F (18° to 27°C) for flower development in the sales area.

Irrigation. Keep plants uniformly moist. Drying out or excessive wetness causes bud drop.

Disorder. Bud drop: This problem may be caused by (1) exposure to ethylene in the display area, (2) exposure to temperatures below 50°F (10°C), (3) maintaining plants in a low light display area, or (4) allowing plants to dry out or overwatering them.

Consumer care

Light. Place plants in an area with 50 to 100 fc (.5 to 1.1 klux) of light. Flowering increases as light levels increase.

Temperature. Maintain plants at indoor temperatures from 65° to 80°F (18° to 27°C) for maximum flowering and minimum bud drop. Avoid temperatures below 50°F (10°C). Plants can be used outdoors on the patio during summer.

Location. Choose an east, west or south window.

Irrigation. Water plants as often as necessary to keep them uniformly moist. Don't overwater or allow them to dry out, or buds will drop.

Grooming. Old flowers should be removed daily.

Disorder. Bud drop: This problem may be caused by several factors under interior conditions including low light, drying out, exposure to cold or hot air drafts, overwatering or high temperatures.

Cultivars. A number of hibiscus cultivars are available, offering a range of flower colors, flower forms and leaf types. All cultivars exhibit sensitivity to ethylene, darkness and low temperatures, but there are differences in sensitivity to bud drop during shipping in some cultivars being introduced to the market. Specific cultivar evaluations have not been conducted.

H

ADDITIONAL READING

Hoyer, L. 1984. Bud, flower and leaf drop in *Hibiscus rosa-sinensis* caused by ethylene and darkness. *Tidsskrift for Planteavl* 88(5):489-501.

Hoyer, L. 1986. Silver thiosulfate can to some extent prevent leaf, bud, and flower drop in *Hibiscus rosa-sinensis* caused by ethylene and darkness. *Acta Horticultura* 181:147-153.

Nell, T.A. and J.E. Barrett. 1984. Effect of simulated shipping temperature duration on prefinished flowering hibiscus. *Proceedings of the Florida State Horticultural Society* 97:278-279.

Rystedt, J. 1982. Effects of high and low temperatures on the subsequent keeping quality of *Hibiscus rosa-sinensis* and Begonia Nixe. *Tidsskrift Planteavl* 86:31-36.

———. 1982. Effects of dark storage on the subsequent keeping quality of *Hibiscus rosa-sinensis* and Begonia Nixe. *Tidsskrift Planteavl* 86:37-46.

Thaxton, D.R. 1986. Determination of factors involved in *Hibiscus rosa-sinensis* L. bud abscission. M.S. thesis, Texas A & M University.

Thaxton, D.R., J.W. Kelly and J.J. Frett. 1988. Control of *Hibiscus rosa-sinensis* L. bud abscission during shipping. *Scientia Horticultura* 34:131-137.

H

Hippeastrum X cv.

hip-ee-*ass*-trum

Family Name: **Amaryllidaceae**
Common Name: **Amaryllis**

South American herb with tunicate bulb. The generic name amaryllis has been applied in the United States to Hippeastrum, from which the amaryllis of horticulture is derived, but historically, and now by international accord, the name is correctly used as it appears here.

AMARYLLIS

Production factors

Nutrition. High quality plants can be produced without fertilizer during production. Some growers apply small amounts of fertilizer, but the longevity effects have not been determined.

Development stage. Sell plants when flower stalk is 12 inches (30 cm) tall and leaves are 6 to 12 inches (15 to 30 cm) long, or when the second bud is visible.

Problems. Diseases: Stagonospora (red spot or fire), Fusarium, Colletotricum and viruses.

Insects: Mites, thrips, mealybugs, woolly aphids and root eelworms.

Postproduction factors

Shipping, handling and storage

Temperature. Because amaryllis are tropical plants that are sensitive to cold temperatures, maintain storage and shipping temperatures above 50°F (10°C).

Lasting qualities. Plants will flower for 14 to 21 days.

Care and grooming. Remove damaged or yellow leaves before sleeving.

Retail handling

Light. Amaryllis may be stored under low light conditions (50 fc; .5 klux) for several days without detrimental effects. Extended storage before sale may result in bud abortion and excessive stem elongation. Bulbs are commonly sold in kits that let consumers plant the bulb before stem elongation. In this case, bulbs are stored in the dark without problems, provided bulbs don't sprout. Bulbs should be sold before sprouting.

H

51

Hippeastrum X cv.

hip-ee-*ass*-trum

Temperature. Store and display plants from 65° to 70°F (18° to 21°C) so that flowers remain in the bud stage until purchase. Plants with open flowers may be easier to market, but open flowers are easily damaged during delivery to the customer and have a shorter life.

Irrigation. Use room temperature water.

Consumer care

Light. Light levels of 50 to 100 fc (.5 to 1.1 klux) are satisfactory. The effects of lower light levels are not known.

Temperature. The interior temperature is more important to the longevity of potted amaryllis than any other factor. Maintain the plants at 65 to 70°F (18° to 21°C). Flowers open more rapidly, and each flower lasts for a shorter time as interior temperatures are increased.

Location. Place the plant in or near a window.

Irrigation. Keep soil moist, but avoid overwatering or letting medium dry out. Fertilize the bulb every 2 to 4 weeks if it's to be reflowered the following year.

Grooming. Flowers will open over a 1 to 2 week period and will die at various times. Remove individual flowers as they wilt.

Reflowering. Amaryllis bulbs can be reflowered each year by the consumer. For best results, grow the plant outdoors after the last chance of frost. Let the plant dry out and bring it indoors for 8 weeks in late summer, then remove the foliage and resume watering.

Cultivars. No comparative information is available regarding the longevity of amaryllis cultivars.

ADDITIONAL READING

De Hertogh, A.A. 1989. Amaryllis (Hippeastrum)—potted plants. *Holland Bulb Forcers Guide*. New York: Netherlands Flower Bulb Institute.

Growing Amaryllis. 1981. London: Grower Books.

Nell, T.A., A.A. De Hertogh and J.E. Barrett. 1991. Bulbs as flowering potted plants—keys to increased longevity. *GrowerTalks* 55(7):57-60.

H

Hyacinthus orientalis

hye-uh-*sin*-thus
or-ee-en-*tay*-liss

Family Name: **Liliaceae**
Common Names: **Hyacinth, Dutch Hyacinth, Common Hyacinth, Garden Hyacinth**

North Africa, Greece to Asia Minor and Syria—one species. A bulbous, perennial herb with tunicate bulb.

ANNE MARIE

Production factors

No information is available on the effects that production cultural practices or environmental conditions have on hyacinth interior longevity.

Development stage. Market plants when the flower bud is first visible.

Problems. Diseases: Penicillium, Botrytis. Insect: Aphids.

Disorder. Dropping of the flower stalk: This disorder—referred to as spitting—is the abortion of the flower stalk from the basal plate. It's commonly a result of the bulbs being frozen in the rooting room.

Postproduction factors

Shipping, handling and storage

Light. Plants can be stored in the dark, provided temperatures are maintained properly. Plants shipped in the dark at 60°F (16°C) or higher may elongate during transit.

Temperature. Store and ship plants at 32° to 35°F (0° to 2°C). Spray plants with a fungicide to protect against Botrytis. Bulbs can be stored at the green bud stage for 4 weeks.

Gases. Avoid ethylene exposure, or flower drop will occur.

Lasting qualities. Flowers last 7 to 14 days.

Care and grooming. Keep foliage dry and medium moist during shipping and storage.

H

Hyacinthus orientalis

hye-uh-*sin*-thus
or-ee-en-*tay*-liss

Retail handling

Light. Display plants at light levels of 50 to 100 fc (.5 to 1.1 klux) or higher. Avoid direct sunlight.

Temperature. Provide cool temperatures of 60° to 68°F (16° to 20°C) during display. Maintaining plants at higher temperatures leads to rapid flower opening and reduced longevity.

Irrigation. Hyacinths don't need large amounts of water. Apply water sparingly, but don't let the medium dry out.

Disorder. Stem topple: The stems of some hyacinth cultivars fall over as the flower stalk increases in length. Apply Ethephon during production to minimize this problem.

Consumer care

Light. Light levels between 50 to 100 fc (.5 to 1.1 klux) are adequate for hyacinth. The plants can be placed in higher light locations, but avoid direct sunlight.

Temperature. Extend longevity by keeping plants in cool temperature areas. Flowers will last 4 to 7 days longer at 65°F (18°C) compared to 80°F (27°C).

Location. Place the plant near any window.

Irrigation. Keep the medium uniformly moist, and avoid drying out.

Grooming. Remove individual flower stalks as needed.

Cultivars. Red, pink, white, blue and violet flower colors are available. No information is available on the longevity differences among cultivars.

ADDITIONAL READING

De Hertogh, A.A. 1985. *Holland Bulb Forcers Guide*. New York: Netherlands Flower Bulb Institute.

———. 1985. Bulbous crops. R.A. Larson, ed. *Introduction to Floriculture*. New York: Academic Press Inc.

Nell, T.A., A.A. De Hertogh and J.E. Barrett. 1991. Bulbs as flowering potted plants—keys to increased longevity. *GrowerTalks* 55(7):57-60.

H

Hydrangea macrophylla

hye-*dran*-jee-uh
mak-roh-*fil*-luh

Family Name: **Saxifragaceae**
Common Names: **Hydrangea, Hortensia**

North and South America and Middle and East Asia—one of 35 species of erect or climbing, deciduous or evergreen shrubs. Most commercial flowering plants are sold for the large, showy flowers consisting primarily of conspicuous petal-like sepals.

BOTTSTEIN

Production factors

No information is available on the effects of production factors on hydrangea interior longevity.

Development stage. Market plants when florets are fully colored but not overly mature. Hydrangeas are sometimes marketed, especially in Europe, with many of the florets still green or only partially colored. These undeveloped bracts will not develop good coloration unless plants are placed in high light areas. The inflorescences on multiflowered plants should be at a similar stage of development at time of sale.

Problems. Diseases: Inflorescence blight, leaf spot, powdery mildew, root rot, Southern blight, stem rot, bacterial wilt, cucumber mosaic, hydrangea ring spot, tobacco ring spot and tomato ring spot.

Insects: Aphids, leaf tiers, rose chafers, scales, tarnished plant bugs, thrips, two-spotted mites, leaf nematodes, root nematodes, stem nematodes and slugs.

Disorders. Numerous nutritional problems that may affect leaf coloration and flower color may occur in hydrangea production. Monitor and maintain medium pH carefully to avoid these problems.

Postproduction factors

Shipping, handling and storage

Light. Keeping plants in the dark for more than 2 to 3 days, depending on temperature can cause hydrangea leaf drop. Specific information on shipping duration isn't known. Store and ship plants in the dark for the shortest possible time to avoid leaf drop problems.

H

Hydrangea macrophylla

hye-*dran*-jee-uh
mak-roh-*fil*-luh

Temperature. Store and ship plants at cool temperatures (35°F; 1°C) to maximize longevity. Plant quality and longevity were reduced following 4 or more days of simulated shipping at 35°F or 2 days at 68°F (20°C). Avoid condensation and possible Botrytis that may occur at low shipping temperatures by cooling the plants before boxing or using a preventative fungicide spray.

Lasting qualities. Plants continue to flower for 21 to 28 days.

Care and grooming. Remove damaged leaves and flowers before plants are sleeved, stored and shipped. Water plants thoroughly and allow them to drain before boxing and shipping.

Retail handling

Light. Provide a light level of 250 fc (2.7 klux) or greater for maximum longevity.

Temperature. Display plants from 60° to 80°F (16° to 27°C) for good results.

Irrigation. Use a large amount of water to avoid wilting of leaves and petals. Severe drying will lead to brown necrotic spots on leaves and florets and leaf drop. Antitranspirants have been evaluated as a means of reducing interior water requirements, but phytotoxicity was observed at rates sufficiently high to reduce water use. Therefore, use of antitranspirants is not currently recommended.

Consumer care

Light. Provide a high light level (250 fc; 2.7 klux) to maximize longevity. Plants will tolerate light levels of 50 to 100 fc (.5 to 1.1 klux), but leaf drop and pale floret color may occur.

Temperature. Keep plants in a cool location, from 65° to 75°F (18° to 24°C).

Location. Place plants near a window that provides high light levels. Avoid direct sunlight so that plants don't dry out rapidly.

Irrigation. Water plants frequently to avoid wilting of leaves and flowers. Hydrangeas can be damaged by overwatering, so it's important to maintain a moist medium without applying water so frequently that overwatering becomes a problem.

Grooming. Remove individual leaves and flowers as needed to keep the plant attractive.

Disorder. Browning of florets: The outer floret margins may become brown and dessicated if plants are allowed to dry out.

Cultivars. A number of cultivars are available offering pink, blue, red, purple and bicolor bracts. A new inflorescence form, Lace Caps, is becoming very popular in Europe and is being introduced into the United States. These plants have dense flower heads with male sterile blooms and a few large petals on the outer perimeter of the inflorescence. No information is available on individual cultivar longevity.

ADDITIONAL READING

Heins, R.D. and J.E. Hanan. 1984. Life after harvest. *Greenhouse Grower.* 2(7):42-46.

Tracy, T.E. and A.J. Lewis. 1981. Effects of antitranspirants on hydrangea. *HortScience* 16:87-89.

Weiler, T.C. 1980. Hydrangeas. R.A. Larson, ed. *Introduction to Floriculture.* New York: Academic Press Inc.

H

Kalanchoe blossfeldiana

ka-*lan*-koh-ee
blos-feld-ee-*ah*-na

Family Name: **Crassulaceae**
Common Name: **Kalanchoe**

Madagascar—about 125 species of succulent perennials or monocarpic herbs or shrubs, mostly of Africa and Madagascar, a few Asiatic or pantropical. The common pot plant is valued for winter flowers that remain fresh for 7 to 8 weeks. Many are listed cultivars.

GOLDSTRIKE

Production factors

No information is available on the effects of production light level and temperature on kalanchoe longevity.

Light. Provide light levels of 5,000 to 6,000 fc (53.8 to 64.6 klux) to produce high-quality plants.

Temperature. Maintain night temperatures at 60° to 67°F (16° to 19°C). Temperatures above 74°F (23°C) delay flowering and reduce quality.

Development stage. Market plants when 10% to 30% of the flowers are open. The remaining flower buds will generally open indoors.

Problems. Diseases: Powdery mildew and crown rot.

Insects: Lepidoptera larvae, aphids, common or citrus mealybugs and whitefly.

Disorder. Flower streaking: Flowers show a white streaking on the petal margins and throughout the flower during production or after plants are indoors. While the exact cause isn't known, it appears that numerous factors including nutrition, light levels and temperature may cause this disorder. Some cultivars don't have this problem.

Postproduction factors

Shipping, handling and storage

Light. Prolonged periods of darkness (3 or more weeks) increase the number of chlorotic leaves, reduce chlorophyll content and plant quality.

Temperature. Maintain a temperature of 40°F (4°C). Plants are more sensitive to ethylene at higher temperatures. Store plants up to 3 weeks, but storage duration should be as short as possible.

Gases. Flowers and buds are sensitive to

K

ethylene. If exposure occurs, buds will not open, and plants will show flower sleepiness, petal fading and desiccation and closing of florets.

Lasting qualities. Plants have excellent longevity, lasting 4 to 5 weeks or longer.

Care and grooming. Remove any damaged leaves or flowers before sleeving plants.

Retail handling

Light. Display plants at 50 fc (.5 klux) or higher.

Temperature. Plants can tolerate a wide range of temperatures, from 45° to 90°F (7° to 32°C). Displaying plants at normal room temperatures is acceptable.

Irrigation. Keep plants moderately moist, watering when medium is dry to the touch.

Disorder. Flower sleepiness: If plants have been exposed to ethylene during shipping, storage or retail handling, the flowers will fail to open and appear dry and faded. Damaged flowers will not recover.

Consumer care

Light. Kalanchoes tolerate low light levels (25 fc; 270 lux) but flower development is best with 100 fc (1.1 klux) or higher.

Temperature. Provide normal home temperatures of 65° to 78°F (18° to 26°C) for continued flowering.

Location. Plants will do well in most interior locations.

Irrigation. Keep kalanchoes moist but not overwatered.

Grooming. Remove older flowers as they fade and new flowers open.

Disorder. Failure of flowers to open: This problem may be caused by ethylene injury or plants being marketed before flowers mature in the greenhouse. Flowers injured by ethylene will appear dried out and faded.

Cultivars. While the interior performance of cultivars has not been evaluated, all cultivars generally show good-to-excellent longevity.

ADDITIONAL READING

Carbonneau, M.C. 1975. Kalanchoes, III. *Illinois State Florists' Assoc. Bul.* 359:2-4.

Marousky, F.J. and B.K. Harbaugh. 1979. Ethylene-induced floret sleepiness in *Kalanchoe blossfeldiana* Poelln. *HortScience* 14(4):505-507.

Marousky, F.J. and B.K. Harbaugh. 1980. Foliar chlorosis of *Kalanchoe blossfeldiana* Poelln. as influenced by temperature, darkness, and ethylene. *Proceedings of the Florida State Horticultural Society* 93:175-178.

Lilium longiflorum

lil-ee-um
long-gih-*flor*-um

Family Name: **Liliaceae**
Common Name: **Easter Lily**

Lui Chiu—between 80 and 90 species of perennial herbs of the north temperate zone. Bulbous, with the bulb scaly, not tunicate, sometimes stoloniferous or rhizomatous.

NELLIE WHITE

Production factors

Light. Low light during flower maturation leads to flower bud abortion. Provide supplemental photosynthetic lighting to reduce this problem.

Temperature. Avoid high production temperatures during flower maturation, or premature bud drop will occur.

Nutrition. Termination of fertilizer prior to marketability enhanced foliar chlorens when plants were stored for three weeks at 35°F (2°C). The effects of fertilizer on plants not receiving a storage treatment have not been established.

Gases. Add CO_2 to the production environment to reduce bud drop.

Development stage. Market Easter lilies when the first flower begins to open.

Problems. Diseases: *Botrytis elliptica, Botrytis cinerea*, Rhizoctonia, Pythium, *Collectotricum lilii, Phytophthora parsitica, Phytophthora cactorlum* and *Aphelemhoides olesistus.*

Insects: Aphids, lily beetle, rove beetle, spotted cucumber beetles, lily weevils, narcissus bulb fly, lesser bulb fly, bulb mites, red banded leaf rollers, garden centipedes, eastern lubber grasshoppers, mealybugs, spotted millipedes, roaches, scales, slugs, stem borers, thrips and white grubs.

Disorders. Bud blasting: This problem may be caused by low light production conditions, high production temperatures, high soluble salts, allowing plants to dry out or root rot.

Bud splitting: An infestation of aphids may cause this disorder.

Bud and flower spotting: Control Botrytis to avoid this problem.

Yellowing of lower foliage: While the exact causes of lower leaf problems are not known, the following factors contribute to this problem: overwatering, root injury, drying out, inadequate and excessive fertilizer, low light, high fluorine levels and excessive growth regulator applications.

L

Lilium longiflorum

Postproduction factors

Shipping, handling and storage

Flowering can be delayed by placing plants in cold storage, but prolonged storage will decrease flower longevity.

Light. Light isn't necessary in storage or shipping if the temperature is within the ranges indicated below.

Temperature. Store plants that flower early for up to 2 weeks at 31°F (-1°C) without lights, or 35° to 50°F (2° to 10°C) with 50 fc (.5 klux) light. The lower storage and shipping temperatures are best. Place plants in coolers when the first buds are swollen. Remove plants *carefully* from the cooler 1 day before marketing, and allow them to warm gradually rather than moving them directly to the greenhouse. Ship plants at 38° to 42°F (3° to 5°C).

Gases. Easter lilies are sensitive to ethylene, and exposure results in premature bud drop. Application of silver thiosulfate at 0.5 to 2 mM reduces storage-induced bud abortion but won't increase floral longevity.

Lasting qualities. Lilies last 6 to 10 days.

Care and grooming. Remove the anthers from the flowers as they begin to open to keep pollen from dropping on the flower. Sleeving is recommended to avoid damage to leaves and flowers. The type of sleeve doesn't affect longevity.

Retail handling

Light. Provide high light (50 to 100 fc; .5 to 1.1 klux) to prevent bud drop.

Temperature. Display plants at temperatures from 65° to 75°F (18° to 24°C).

Irrigation. Keep plants moist to prevent bud and lower leaf drop.

Disorders. Bud drop: This problem is caused by low light conditions or drying out.

Leaf drop: Lower leaves will drop if plants dry out, often from excessive storage periods before marketing or shipping at high temperatures.

Consumer care

Light. Keep plants in a high (50 to 100 fc; .5 to 1.1 klux) light area.

Temperature. Provide 65° to 75°F (18° to 24°C) temperatures.

Location. Place plants in an east, south or west window or in an atrium for maximum flower life. Avoid direct sunlight.

Irrigation. Water plants regularly to avoid drying out, but don't overwater.

Grooming. Remove all dead flowers.

Disorder. Failure of buds to open: This may be caused by numerous factors, but placing plants in a low light area prevents immature buds from opening.

Cultivars. The two primary commercial cultivars—Ace and Nellie White—show similar longevity.

L

Lilium longiflorum

lil-ee-um
long-gih-*flor*-um

ADDITIONAL READING

Healy, W.E., R.D. Heins and H.F. Wilkins. 1979. Short-term storage of *Lilium longiflorum* Thunb. Plants in the "puffy" flower bud stage of development. *Minnesota State Florists Bulletin* February.

Kamerbeek, G.A. and A.J.B. Durieux. 1971. Influence of light on flower bud abscission in plants of the lily cultivar Enchantment. *Acta Horticultura* 23:71-74.

Kelley, J.D. and A.I. Schlamp. 1964. Keeping quality, flower size and flowering response of three varieties of Easter lilies to gibberellic acid. *Journal of the American Society of Horticultural Science* 85:631-634.

Prince, T.A., M.S. Cunningham and J.S. Peary. 1987. Floral and foliar quality of potted Easter lilies after STS or phenidone application, refrigerated storage and simulated shipment. *Journal of the American Society of Horticultural Science* 112:469-473.

Prince, T.A. and M.S. Cunningham. 1989. Production and storage factors influencing quality of potted Easter lilies. *HortScience* 24:992-994.

Rees, A.R. 1985. Lilium. A.H. Halevy, ed. *Handbook of Flowering, Vol. 1*. Boca Raton, FL: CRC Press.

Roh, S.M. and H.F. Wilkins. 1977. Temperature and photoperiod effect on flower numbers in *Lilium longiflorum* Thunb. *Journal of the American Society of Horticultural Science* 102:235-242.

Staby, G.L. and T.D. Erwin. 1977. The storage of Easter lilies. *Florists' Review* 161(4162):38.

L

Muscari armeniacum

mus-*kar*-eye
ar-men-ee-*ak*-um

Family Name: **Liliaceae**
Common Name: **Grape Hyacinth**

Mediterranean and Southwest Asia—about 40 species of bulbous, scapose, spring-flowering perennial herbs.

GRAPE HYACINTH

Production factors

No information is available on the effects of production light or temperature levels, media or nutrition on potted grape hyacinth longevity.

Development stage. Market plants when florets are beginning to open. Flower color will be faded if plants are marketed too early, and interior longevity will decrease if marketed after flowers are beginning to open.

Problems. Diseases: Problems are usually avoided by using clean, nondiseased bulbs. Insects: Aphids.

Postproduction factors

Shipping, handling and storage
Light. Plants can be stored and shipped in the dark if temperature is correct.

Temperature. Plants can be stored for several days at 32° to 35°F (0° to 2°C) at the first sign of floret color.

Lasting qualities. Flowers will last 2 to 3 weeks, depending on interior conditions.

Care and grooming. Remove damaged inflorescences before plants are sleeved and shipped to the retailer.

Retail handling

Light. Plants can tolerate a wide range of display light levels. Maintain 50 to 100 fc (.5 to 1.1 klux) or higher for best results.

Temperature. Grape hyacinth *must* be displayed at cool temperatures to avoid rapid flower opening and maximize longevity. Provide temperatures of 60° to 68°F (16° to 20°C).

Irrigation. Keep plants moist at all times.

Consumer care

Light. Light levels as low as 50 fc (.5 klux) have not affected the lifespan or flower elongation of grape hyacinth. Plants can be placed in areas providing 50 fc or higher without problem. Avoid direct sunlight.

Temperature. Because the lifespan of grape hyacinth depends on interior temperature, plants should be used in locations with temperatures between 65° to 70°F (18° to 21°C). Plants maintained at 65°F (18°C) last 7 to 10 days longer than those at 80°F (27°C).

Location. Choose an east, west, south or north window.

Irrigation. Water plants carefully to maintain a uniformly moist medium, and avoid overwatering and drying out.

Grooming. Remove individual flower spikes as needed to keep plants attractive.

Cultivars. Blue Spike and Early Giant are the primary cultivars for potted plant production. No information is available on differences in the longevity of these cultivars.

ADDITIONAL READING

De Hertogh, A.A. 1985. *Holland Bulb Forcers Guide.* New York: Netherlands Flower Bulb Institute.

De Hertogh, A.A. 1985. Bulbous crops. R.A. Larson, ed. *Introduction to Floriculture.* New York: Academic Press Inc.

Nell, T.A., A.A. De Hertogh and J.E. Barrett. 1991. Bulbs as flowering potted plants—keys to increased longevity. *GrowerTalks* 55(7):57-60.

M

Narcissus spp.

nar-*siss*-us

Family Name: **Amaryllidaceae**
Common Names: **Narcissus, Daffodil**

Europe and North Africa—about 26 species of spring or autumn-flowering herbs with tunicate bulbs. Hybridized in nature, narcissus have long been the subject of horticultural hybridization and selection. There are hundreds of named cultivars.

Tête à Tête

Production factors

No information is available on the effects of production light level, temperature, media or nutrition on narcissus longevity.

Development stage. Market plants at the pencil or gooseneck stage. Don't keep them in the greenhouse or storage facility until the buds are showing color, as the plants are difficult to ship and longevity is reduced if they are marketed when flowers are open.

Problems. Diseases: Botrytis, Fusarium. Insects: Aphids.

Postproduction factors

Shipping, handling and storage

Light. Plants will tolerate darkness during shipping to retail markets. Current information suggests that temperature has more effect during shipping than light.

Temperature. Avoid shipping and storage periods longer than 3 to 4 days. If storage is necessary, place plants in a 35° to 41°F (2° to 5°C) cooler when flowers are visible. Don't wait until flowers are showing color to store or ship.

Lasting qualities. Flowers last for 4 to 7 days, depending on the interior conditions and cultivar.

Care and grooming. Remove individual flowers as needed.

Retail handling

Light. Display plants at light levels of 50 to 100 fc (.5 to 1.1 klux).

Temperature. Keep plants cool throughout the marketing chain to maximize longevity for the consumer. Ideally, plants should be displayed at 40° to 45°F (4° to 7°C) until purchased.

Irrigation. Water as needed to keep plants moist.

N

Narcissus spp.

nar-*siss*-us

Consumer care

Light. Longevity can be extended by 1 to 2 days by keeping plants at light levels of 100 fc (1.1 klux), compared to 25 fc (270 lux).

Temperature. Keep plants at 65°F (18°C). Plants will tolerate cooler temperatures, and lifespan may be extended if temperature is lowered. Recent results have demonstrated that plants held at 65°F (18°C) lasted 4 to 5 days longer than those at 80°F (27°C).

Location. Place plants near a window with cool temperatures and bright light.

Irrigation. Keep plants uniformly moist.

Grooming. Remove individual flowers as needed.

Cultivars. While numerous cultivars are available, their longevity has not been identified.

ADDITIONAL READING

De Hertogh, A.A. 1985a. *Holland Bulb Forcers Guide*. New York: Netherlands Flower Bulb Institute.

———. 1985b. Bulbous crops. R.A. Larson, ed. *Introduction to Floriculture*. New York: Academic Press Inc.

Nell, T.A., A.A. De Hertogh and J.E. Barrett. 1991. Bulbs as flowering potted plants—keys to increased longevity. *GrowerTalks* 55(7):57-60.

N

Oxalis spp.

ox-*al*-is

Also: *Oxalis regnellii, Oxalis bowiei, Oxalis deppei,*
Oxalis hirta, Oxalis martiana
Family Name: **Oxalidaceae**
Common Names: **Oxalis, Wood Sorrel, Lady's Sorrel**

South Africa and South America—about 850 species of herbs and suffrutescent plants of all continents; perennial or annual herbs, often bulbous, tuberous or rhizomatous. These plants are grown as ornamentals for bloom in late winter or early spring in window gardens and conservatories.

OXALIS

Production factors

No information is available on the effects of production factors on oxalis longevity.

Development stage. Market plants when they have reached a salable size, as flowers will develop once plants are in the interior.

Problem. Insect: Mites.

Postproduction factors

Shipping, handling and storage

No information is available on the optimum conditions for shipping or problems encountered during the storage and shipping of oxalis.

Retail handling and consumer care

No information is available on the effects of interior conditions required to maximize the interior longevity of oxalis.

Cultivars. Various species or groups of oxalis are available year-round, offering flower colors of white, rose, rose pink and lavender. Longevity differences between species and cultivars aren't known.

ADDITIONAL READING
De Hertogh. A.A. 1985. *Holland Bulb Forcers Guide.*
New York: Netherlands Flower Bulb Institute.

Pelargonium X *domesticum*

pel-ar-*goh*-nee-um
doh-*mes*-tee-kum

Family Name: **Geraniaceae**
Common Name: **Regal Geranium**

South Africa—perennial herbs or shrubs with entire, lobed or dissected leaves. The flowers are irregular, set in an umbel inflorescence.

REGAL GERANIUM

Production factors

No information is available on the effects of production temperature, media or fertilization on Regal geranium longevity.

Light. Plant quality—as determined by the number of flowers opening after plants were moved indoors and the length of flowering period indoors—was greater on plants grown at 1,250 fc (12.5 klux), compared to 2,250 fc (22.5 klux).

Problems. Petal abscission: Petal dropping during and after shipping limits the marketability of Regal geraniums. This problem is most commonly associated with cultivar selection, high shipping temperatures and exposure to ethylene.

Postproduction factors

Shipping, handling and storage

Light. The plants can be shipped in closed boxes. Maximum shipping times have not been established.

Temperature. Ship plants at 42°F (5°C). Petal abscission is a more serious problem at higher shipping temperatures.

Gases. Petal drop is promoted by exposure to low levels of ethylene, even for short periods. Apply a concentration of 175 ppm silver thiosulfate at the first sign of color to reduce petal drop.

Lasting qualities. Plants continue flowering for 2 to 4 weeks indoors.

Grooming. Remove all damaged or diseased leaves before shipping.

Retail handling

Light. Use light levels of 100 fc (1.1 klux) or higher to minimize leaf yellowing and petal abscission during display.

Temperature. Display Regal geraniums

P

Pelargonium ✕ *domesticum*

pel-ar-*goh*-nee-um
doh-*mes*-tee-kum

between 60° to 70°F (16° to 20°C). Plants will tolerate cooler (45° to 50°F; 7° to 10°C) temperatures.

Irrigation. Keep plants moist.

Disorder. Petal abscission: This disorder is a symptom of exposure to ethylene during shipping or display. *Don't expose Regal geraniums to any sources of ethylene*, as this is one of the most sensitive plants to this odorless gas.

Consumer care

Light. While plants will continue to flower at light levels of 50 fc (.5 klux) or higher, plant performance is best with the highest possible light levels. New flowers don't develop at light levels of 25 fc (270 lux) or lower.

Temperature. Provide temperatures of 68° to 72°F (20° to 22°C). Higher temperatures may cause leaf yellowing, petal abscission and reduced longevity.

Location. Choose a bright sunny location for optimum performance indoors.

Irrigation. Keep plants uniformly moist at all times. Avoid overwatering, which results in leaf yellowing and decline of the plant.

Grooming. Remove individual flowers as they fade.

Cultivars. A wide range of flower colors is available. Differences exist in cultivar response, interior performance and ethylene sensitivity, but these are not currently documented.

ADDITIONAL READING

Deneke, C.F. 1988. "The post-harvest quality of *Pelargonium* ✕ *domesticum* L.H. Bailey." Ph.D. dissertation, Pennsylvania State University.

Deneke, C.F., K.B. Evensen and R. Craig. 1990. Regulation of petal abscission in *Pelargonium* ✕ *domesticum. HortScience* 25:937-940.

Olson, K.M. and K.B. Evensen. 1989. The influence of irradiance on ethylene sensitivity and postproduction quality of *Pelargonium* ✕ *domesticum.* University Park, PA: Pennsylvania State University. (In press.)

P

68

Flowering Potted Plants *Pelargonium*

Rhipsalidopsis gaertneri

rip-sal-i-*dop*-sis
gairt-na-ree

Also: **Rhipsalidopsis rosea**
Family Name: **Cactaceae**
Common Name: **Easter Cactus, Spring Cactus**

Brazil—two species of epiphytic cacti. Plants consist of jointed, branched, modified stems. The older stems become 3 to 6 angled, and the upper stems are flat. Flowers are symmetrical.

HEATHER

Production factors

No information is available on the effects of production light level, temperature, nutrition or medium on Easter cacti performance during shipping or in the interior environment.

Development stage. Market plants when flower buds are showing color but before flowers are open, as open flowers bruise easily during handling and shipping.

Problems. Diseases: Root and stem rots caused by Phytophthora or Pythium.

Insects: Mealybugs, scale and thrips.

Disorder. Failure of plants to flower. Easter cacti are short-day plants, and proper temperature and photoperiod are necessary during summer and fall months to form buds. High temperatures or light levels during forcing will cause buds to drop during this period.

Postproduction factors

Shipping, handling and storage
Light. Don't store plants for more than 3 days in the dark.

Temperature. Optimum shipping temperatures are 50° to 60°F (10° to 16°C). Chilling injury may occur at lower temperatures, and bud drop will occur rapidly at temperatures above 80°F (27°C).

Gases. Flowers and flower buds drop when plants are exposed to ethylene. Apply silver thiosulfate to reduce ethylene-induced bud drop.

Lasting qualities. Plants continue flowering for 4 to 6 weeks.

Care and grooming. Remove broken buds and cladophylls before shipping. Don't sell plants with few buds, open flowers or irregular growth.

R

Rhipsalidopsis gaertneri rip-sal-i-*dop*-sis *gairt*-na-ree

Retail handling

Light. Display plants in an area providing light levels of 100 fc (1.1 klux) or higher.

Temperature. Select an area with temperatures between 65° to 70°F (18° to 21°C). Temperatures above 80°F (27°C) and below 50°F (10°C) cause flower drop.

Irrigation. Flower drop occurs if plants dry out; entire plants will wilt and die if overwatered.

Disorder. Flower drop: Bud and flower drop may be caused by exposure to ethylene, exposure to high temperatures, drying out, overwatering or low light conditions.

Consumer care

Light. Choose an area with light levels of 100 fc (1.1 klux) or higher to prevent bud drop. Avoid direct sunlight.

Temperature. Place plants in a location with temperatures between 65° to 75°F (18° to 24°C).

Irrigation. Keep plants uniformly moist to avoid flower drop caused by drying out or overwatering.

Grooming. Remove individual flowers as they die.

Disorder. Flower drop: See *Retail handling,* above.

Cultivars. Some excellent cultivars are available, offering a range of red, pink, purple and white flower colors. No information is available on the interior performance of these cultivars.

ADDITIONAL READING
Boyle, T.H., D.J. Jacques and D.P. Stimart. 1988. Influence of photoperiod and growth regulators on flowering of *Rhipsalidopsis gaertneri. Journal of the American Society of Horticultural Science* 113(1):75-78.
Nell, T.A. 1988. Easter cactus—a new crop for American growers. *GrowerTalks* 52(5):84, 86, 88.
Wilkins, H.F. and W. Runger. 1985. Rhipsalidopsis. A.H. Halevy, ed. *Handbook of Flowering, Vol. IV.* Boca Raton, FL: CRC Press Inc.

R

Rhododendron spp.　　roh-doh-*den*-dron

Family Name: **Ericaceae**
Common Name: **Azalea, Rhododendron**

Japan—perhaps 800 species of evergreen, semi-evergreen or deciduous shrubs or rarely small trees or epiphytes. Most abundant in the Himalayas, Southeast Asia and mountains of Malaysia, but found on all continents except Africa and South America.

AZALEA

Production factors

Light. Forcing at light levels below 2,500 fc (26.9 klux) reduces number of flowers, increases number of days to flowering, and decreases intensity of flower color in red, pink and variegated cultivars.

Temperature. Maintain temperatures that promote floral initiation and development to avoid uneven bud development. Interior longevity is increased and flower color is intensified at day/night temperatures of 65°/60°F (18°/16°C), compared to higher production temperatures (85°/80°F; 29°/27°C). Time to flowering is extended at lower temperatures.

Nutrition. Stop fertilizing 2 to 4 weeks before cooling to reduce brown leaves during and after cooling. Flower color is darker, and longevity is best when no fertilizer is used during forcing.

Irrigation. Avoid drying out during forcing, or flower abortion and uneven flowering will occur.

Development stage. Market plants with 25% to 30% of the flowers open at time of sale. Plants can be sold before this stage, but the color of the flowers that open indoors is pale and the overall plant quality is reduced.

Problems. Diseases: Phytophthora, Cylindrocladium, Botrytis, petal blight, leaf gall, septoria leaf spot and powdery mildew.

Insects: Azalea lace bugs, leaf miners, leaf rollers, aphids, thrips, whitefly, southern red mites, two-spotted mites, stylet nematodes, stunt nematodes and root knot nematodes.

Disorders. Nonuniform flowering: This problem may be caused by pinching late, beginning the dormancy-breaking treatment too early, providing low light or drying out during forcing or marketing the plants too early.

Defoliation: Leaves may drop on plants cooled in facilities contaminated with ethylene or in coolers with low humidity

R

(less than 70% relative humidity). There may also be problems if plants are cooled above 40°F (4°C) without lights. Lighting must be above 30 fc (322 lux) if plants are to be cooled at 48°F (9°C) without brown leaves and bud abortion occurring.

Postproduction factors

Shipping, handling and storage

Light. Not necessary in shipping or storage periods less than 7 days.

Temperature. Ship and store the plants at 35° to 40°F (2° to 4°C) to avoid problems with brown leaves and bud abortion.

Gases. Exposure to ethylene causes defoliation, especially during cooling.

Lasting qualities. Azaleas have an excellent lifespan, lasting 3 to 4 weeks.

Care and grooming. Remove damaged or diseased leaves and flowers before plants are sleeved and boxed. Because azaleas are commonly grown in peat-based media that dries out rapidly, plants should be moist at time of boxing. However, avoid watering immediately before boxing since excess moisture in the shipping boxes may lead to disease on flowers and foliage.

Retail handling

Light. Display plants in areas with 35 fc (377 lux) or more of light.

Temperature. Keep plants in cool (68° to 72°F; 20° to 22°C) areas for the best quality.

Irrigation. Check wetness of medium when plants are unboxed. Add water if needed to provide a moist medium during display. Don't let plants dry out or longevity will be reduced.

Disorder. Bruising of petals: Damage to petals may occur during transit if plants are not sleeved or if plants are sleeved with too many open flowers.

Consumer care

Light. Azalea longevity is not affected by normal indoor light levels (50 to 100 fc; .5 to 1.1 klux). Avoid direct sunlight since plants will dry out rapidly and damage may occur on the flowers and leaves.

Temperature. Maintain plants in cool (68° to 72°F; 20° to 22°C) areas.

Location. Place plants near a window but out of direct sunlight.

Irrigation. Keep plants uniformly moist at all times. If plants do become dry, it may be necessary to submerge the entire root system in water to thoroughly rewet the peat moss-based media. Drying out will greatly reduce the longevity of most cultivars.

Grooming. Remove dead flowers as needed.

Disorder. Faded flowers: Flowers that are just showing color when placed into the interior will develop into pale colored flowers. Only purchase plants with more open flowers, or place plants in higher light levels.

Cultivars. A number of cultivars—most with excellent longevity—are available with red, pink, white and variegated flowers. Some differences exist in flower drop and sensitivity to drying out. Redwing will drop flowers following poor handling and show petal burn if plants dry out.

R

Rhododendron spp.

roh-doh-*den*-dron

ADDITIONAL READING

Black, L.A. 1989. "Postharvest performance of Gloria azalea as affected by factors during forcing and simulated transport and by dormancy breaking method." M.S. thesis, University of Florida.

Black, L.A., T.A. Nell and J.E. Barrett. 1990. Dormancy-breaking method effects on azalea longevity. *HortScience* 25:810.

———. 1991. Postproduction performance of Gloria azalea in response to flower maturity and simulated transport. *HortScience* 25:571-574.

Larson, R.A. 1980. Azaleas. R.A. Larson, ed. *Introduction to Floriculture*. New York: Academic Press.

———. 1975. Continuous production of flowering azaleas. A.M. Kofranek and R.A. Larson, eds. *Growing Azaleas Commercially*. Berkeley, CA: University of California.

Stadtherr, R.J. 1975. Commercial cultivars. A.M. Kofranek and R.A. Larson, eds. *Growing Azaleas Commercially*. Berkeley, CA: University of California.

Sterling, E.P. and W.H. Molenaar. 1985. *Transport tolerantie van potplanten. Mededeling Nr. 39*. Wageningen: The Netherlands: Sprenger Institute.

R

Rosa X *hybrida*

ro-sa *hye*-brih-dah

Family Name: **Rosaceae**
Common Name: **Pot Rose**

Mexico—Many species have been modified through selection and hybridization in cultivation, giving rise to some 20,000 cultivars.

MINIATURE POT ROSES

Production factors

No information is available on the effects of production light level, temperature, media or nutrition on interior longevity for pot roses.

Development stage. Market plants when five to six flowers are open and numerous buds are showing color. Tight buds may not open on some cultivars once plants are moved indoors.

Problems. Diseases: Black spot, Botrytis, crown gall, downy mildew, powdery mildew, rust, viruses.

Insects: Aphids, leaf rollers, thrips and two-spotted spider mite.

Disorder. Leaf drop: Numerous causes are known for this disorder including drying out; exposure to ethylene, sulfur dioxide, or ammonium, and foliar diseases.

Postproduction factors

Shipping, handling and storage

Light. Pot roses are very sensitive to darkness. Avoid prolonged periods of darkness during shipping and handling that can cause leaf and flower drop. Plants should be shipped for a maximum of 6 days in the dark, depending on temperature.

Temperature. Maintain shipping and storing temperatures of 34°F (1°C) to 41°F (5°C) to reduce or eliminate leaf and flower drop. Higher temperatures lead to bud drop, leaf yellowing and drop, and failure of the plant to develop additional flowers in interior locations.

Gases. Pot roses are sensitive to ethylene, and exposure should be avoided. Maintain shipping and holding temperatures of 34° to 41°F (1° to 5°C) to reduce ethylene effects

R

during production.

Lasting qualities. Plants may continue to flower indoors for 6 to 7 weeks if handled properly during shipping and given high interior light levels.

Care and grooming. Remove damaged foliage and flowers before shipping. Be sure to grade plants for uniformity, number of flowers and other factors needed to establish their marketability.

Retail handling

Light. Display plants at 100 fc (1.1 klux) of light or higher to assure that flowers develop properly once they are purchased by the consumer. Lower light levels in the display area, even for brief periods, promote bud drop.

Temperature. Maintain temperatures of 65° to 70°F (18° to 21°C).

Irrigation. Keep medium uniformly moist to avoid leaf and flower drop.

Disorders. Leaf and flower drop: These problems are common on plants that have been shipped at warm temperatures (60°F [16°C] or higher) or for prolonged periods. Maintaining plants in low light conditions or exposing plants to ethylene in the retail display can also lead to these problems.

Failure of buds to develop: This is commonly caused by improper shipping conditions, exposure to ethylene or keeping the plants under low light conditions.

Consumer care

Light. Provide good light conditions. Orange Rosamini plants continued to flower for 7 weeks at 100 fc (1.1 klux) compared to 2 weeks when maintained at 25 fc (270 lux). Light levels greater than 100 fc can be used, but avoid direct sunlight.

Temperature. Provide cool (65° to 70°F; 18° to 21°C) temperatures for the best interior quality. Plants can be exposed to temperatures of 40°F (4°C) without problems; temperatures higher than 80°F (27°C) lead to reduced flowering and decreased longevity.

Location. Select an east, south, or west window. Avoid direct sunlight.

Irrigation. Keep potted roses moist at all times. Drying out leads to leaf yellowing and drop.

Grooming. Remove old flowers as they fade.

Disorder. Leaf yellowing and drop: This problem is caused by placing the plants in low light conditions or allowing them to dry out in the interior.

Cultivars. Numerous cultivars are available. Red Garnette and Orange Margo Koster are more tolerant of shipping conditions than Pink Margo Koster. Some pot rose cultivars are more tolerant to interior conditions than others, but a comprehensive evaluation of current cultivars' performance hasn't been conducted.

ADDITIONAL READING

Halevy, A.H. and A.M. Kofranek. 1976. The prevention of flower bud and leaf abscission in pot roses during simulated transport. *Journal of the American Society of Horticultural Science* 101(6):658-660.

Maxie, E.C., R.F. Hasek and R.H. Sciaroni. 1974. Keep potted roses cool. *Flower and Nursery Rep.* University of California. March, pp. 9-10.

Nell, T.A. and C.V. Noordegraaf. 1991. Simulated-transport temperature and duration and postproduction irradiance level influence postproduction performance of potted roses. *HortScience* 26. (1401-1404).

Nell, T.A. and C.V. Noordegraaf. 1992. Postproduction performance of potted rose under simulated transport and low irradiance levels. *HortScience* 27:239-241.

R

Saintpaulia ionantha

saint-*paul*-ee-uh
eye-oh-*nan*-thuh

Family Name: **Gesneriaceae**
Common Name: **African Violet**

East Africa—about 21 species of terrestrial, perennial, hairy herbs. This popular pot plant has numerous cultivars.

OPTIMARA ASSORTMENT

Production factors

No information is available on the effects of production environmental conditions or cultural factors on African violet interior longevity.

Problems. Diseases: Botrÿtis, crown rot, leaf black rot, leafy gall and powdery mildew.

Insects: Aphids, cyclamen mites, mealybugs, root-knot nematodes and foliar nematodes.

Disorder. Yellow leaves: This problem may be a result of producing plants under high light conditions (above 1,300 fc [14 klux]), keeping them too wet or improper fertilization levels.

Postproduction factors

Shipping, handling and storage

Light. These plants can tolerate shipping or storage in the dark; however, the length of time they can be stored without a loss of quality or longevity is not known.

Temperature. African violets are sensitive to chilling temperatures. Don't expose plants to temperatures below 50°F (10°C) or above 70°F (21°C). Exposure to temperatures outside of this range may result in rapid flower opening, wilted and brown leaves and flowers, brown flower margins or rapid fading of the flowers.

Lasting qualities. Plants have an excellent lifespan and will continue to flower indoors if they are maintained properly.

Care and grooming. African violets are difficult to sleeve without breaking the leaves.

Retail handling

Light. Place plants in good light conditions of 50 to 100 fc (.5 to 1.1 klux) so that some of the flower buds open for best display. African violets are tolerant of low light levels for brief periods.

Saintpaulia ionantha

saint-*paul*-ee-uh
eye-oh-*nan*-thuh

Temperature. Display plants at temperatures between 50° and 75°F (10° and 24°C) to avoid rapid flower opening and brown leaves and to prevent chilling injury on flowers.

Irrigation. Water plants with tepid water from the bottom of the pot. Avoid watering the leaves or there may be permanent leaf spotting.

Disorders. Flower bruising: This is caused by mechanical injury, especially on white-flowered cultivars.

Ring/leaf spot: Hot or cold water on the leaves causes irregular spotting. Avoid a temperature difference of more than 14°F (8°C) between the air and the water.

Consumer care

Light. Plants tolerate low light conditions and will continue to flower for 12 months or longer when given 20 fc (215 lux) of light for 12 hours per day. The number of new flowers and leaves increases with higher light levels or longer lighting duration.

Temperature. Provide interior growing temperatures of 65° to 70°F (18° to 21°C). Avoid temperatures below 50°F (10°C) and above 75°F (24°C).

Location. Choose an east or west window. Don't place plants in direct sunlight.

Irrigation. Apply room temperature water from the bottom of the pot, being careful not to wet the leaves or flowers. Avoid overwatering, which causes root injury and reduced longevity, as well as drying out.

Grooming. Remove dead flowers and flower stalks.

Disorder. Ring spot: See *Retail handling*, above.

Cultivars. Hundreds of cultivars are available. Those introduced in the last 10 years have established new standards for African violets in the interior. These cultivars, including Ballet and Optimara types, offer plants that produce large, long-lasting flowers indoors.

ADDITIONAL READING

Conover, C.A. and R.T. Poole. 1981. Light. acclimatization of African violet. *HortScience* 16:92-93.

Elliott, F.H. 1946. Saintpaulia leaf spot and temperature differential. *Proceedings of the American Society of Horticultural Science* 47:511-514.

Kimmins, R.K. 1980. Gloxinias, African violets, and other Gesneriads. R.A. Larson, ed. *Introduction to Floriculture*. New York: Academic Press Inc.

Poesch, G.W. 1940. Tests show Saintpaulia ring spot caused by cold water. *Florists' Review* 87:21.

Sterling, E.P. and W.H. Molenaar. 1985. *Transport tolerantie van potplanten. Mededeling Nr. 39* Wageningen, The Netherlands: Sprenger Institute.

S

Schlumbergera bridgesii

shlum-*ber*-ger-uh
bri-*jez*-ee-ee

Also: ***Schlumbergera truncata***
Family Name: **Cactaceae**
Common Names: **Christmas Cactus, Crab Cactus, Claw Cactus, Yoke Cactus, Spring Cactus, Thanksgiving Cactus, Linkleaf**

Brazil—Three species of epiphytic cacti with flat-jointed stems. These cultivars are commonly grown as window or conservatory plants for their abundant flowers in winter.

CHRISTMAS FANTASY

Production factors

Low energy requirements and efficient use of space make Christmas and Thanksgiving cacti a popular fall-season crop among commercial producers. However, no information is available on the effects of production temperature, light, media or nutrition on the interior performance of these cacti.

Development stage. Market plants when flowers are showing color but before they are open. Open flowers bruise easily during handling and shipping.

Problems. Diseases: Root and stem rots caused by Phytophthora, Pythium or Rhizoctonia.

Insects: Mealybugs, scale and thrips.

Disorder. Failure of plants to flower: Christmas and Thanksgiving cacti are short-day plants and will not flower with a day length greater than 9 to 12 hours.

Postproduction factors

Shipping, handling and storage

Temperature. Provide storage and shipping temperatures of 50° to 60°F (10° to 16°C). Plants exposed to lower temperatures will drop their flowers, buds and cladophylls (flattened foliaceous stems).

Gases. Flowers and flower buds drop when plants are exposed to ethylene. Applications of silver thiosulfate have been highly effective in preventing ethylene's detrimental effects. Bud length at flowering is shorter on silver thiosulfate-treated plants. The longevity of treated plants may be affected

S

Schlumbergera bridgesii

shlum-*ber*-ger-uh
bri-*jez*-ee-ee

slightly but not significantly enough to be noticed by consumers. Silver thiosulfate can be purchased as a premixed solution or made according to the following formula:

(1) Dissolve either 60 grams of prismatic thiosulfate or 40 grams of anhydrous sodium thiosulfate in 236 ml (1 cup) of deionized or distilled water.

(2) In a separate container, dissolve 10 grams of silver nitrate and add deionized or distilled water to make a solution containing a final volume of 236 ml (1 cup).

(3) Pour the silver nitrate stock solution into the sodium thiosulfate solution. The solutions must be stored rapidly as they are mixed.

(4) Store stock solution in a glass or plastic container in the dark in a refrigerator.

(5) To prepare the final solution, measure 60 ml (2 ounces) of the stock solution and dilute with 3.785 liters (1 gallon) of water. A spreader-sticker should be added as recommended by the manufacturer.

(6) The silver thiosulfate solution should be applied 2 to 4 weeks before marketing.

It may be easier to use a prepared mix of silver thiosulfate; numerous good commercial formulations are available. Evaluate manufacturers' rates on cactus before applying to the entire crop.

Lasting qualities. Plants will continue flowering for 4 to 6 weeks.

Care and grooming. Grade plants to assure good bud count and plant uniformity. Discard any plants with damaged buds or cladophylls, or use them for stock plant material.

Retail handling

Light. These fall season plants are sensitive to low light conditions. Display plants in areas with 50 to 100 fc (.5 to 1.1 klux) of light, or buds will fail to open when transferred to interior settings.

Temperature. Maintain plants at temperatures between 60° to 70°F (16° to 20°C). Exposure to temperatures below 50°F (10°C) leads to chilling injury and bud drop.

Irrigation. Because these cacti don't require large amounts of water, avoid overwatering. However, the flowers and buds will drop if plants become too dry.

Disorder. Flower drop: This problem occurs if plants are exposed to ethylene, exposed to high (80°F; 27°C) or low (less than 50°F [10°C]) temperatures, allowed to dry out, overwatered or placed under low light conditions during display for 4 days or more.

Consumer care

Light. Provide a well-lighted area with 100 fc (1.1 klux) of light from natural or artificial sources. Buds will drop if light levels are too low.

Location. Choose an east, south or west window.

Irrigation. Keep plants uniformly moist to avoid flower drop.

Grooming. These cacti will bloom over a 4- to 6-week period, and some flowers will begin to die as others are opening. Remove the old flowers to maintain an attractive potted plant.

S

Disorder. Flower drop: See *Retail handling*.

Reflowering. Place plants outdoors in indirect light during the summer months, and apply moderate amounts of water and fertilizer. Stop watering at the end of summer and hold plants at temperatures near 50°F (10°C) until flower buds appear in late October. Then increase temperature to 60°F (16°C) until flowering. Higher temperatures may prevent flower buds from developing.

Cultivars. A number of new cultivars have been introduced to markets in the United States and Europe in recent years, offering a range of flower colors including red, pink and yellow. Cultivars vary in response to low light interior conditions. Under interior testing conditions in Holland, Evita and Nicole had more flowers to open under interior conditions than Gold Charm. Information on the interior performance of other cultivars is not available.

ADDITIONAL READING

Boyle, T.H. 1989. "Use of silver thiosulfate on holiday cacti to reduce flower and bud drop." University of Massachusetts (handout).

Cameron, A.C. and M.S. Reid. 1981. The use of silver thiosulfate anionic complex as a foliar spray to prevent flower abscission of zygocactus. *HortScience* 16:761-762.

———. 1983. Use of silver thiosulfate to prevent flower abscission from potted plants. *Scientia Horticultura* 19:373-378.

Cameron, A.C., M.S. Reid and G.W. Hickman. 1983. A silver spray keeps potted flowering plants from shattering. *Florist's Review* 172(4461):59-60.

Hammer, P.A. 1980. Other flowering potted plants. R.A. Larson, ed. *Introduction to Floriculture*. New York: Academic Press Inc.

S

Senecio × *hybridus*

seh-*nee*-kee-oh
hye-brih-dus

Family Name: **Jacobaea**
Common Names: **Cineraria, Florist's Cineraria**

Canary Islands—one of the largest genera of flowering plants, variously esti-mated at 2,000 to 3,000 species, in all parts of the world. Annual or perennial herbs or shrubs. The cineraria produced by florists is often grown under glass for its abundant flowers in many colors.

CINDY

Production factors

No information is available on the effects of production factors on cineraria longevity.

Irrigation. Cineraria require large amounts of water. Antitranspirants will reduce water use during production, but results have been inconsistent and some phytotoxicity has occurred following applications. Moisture absorbents have not reduced water use during production.

Stage of development. Market plants when five to six flowers are open, and the flower buds are visible and well developed, preferably showing color.

Problems. Diseases: Botrytis and pow-dery mildew.

Insects: Aphids, leaf miners and whitefly.

Disorder. Failure of plants to flower: Plants may fail to flower, or flowering may not be uniform if they don't receive a low-temperature (below 59°F [15°C]) period.

Postproduction factors

Shipping, handling and storage

Temperature. Ship cineraria at 40° to 45°F (4° to 7°C) for no more than 3 days. Pack plants at cool temperatures so conden-sation doesn't form on leaves and flowers as plants are cooled in a closed box. Condensa-tion may lead to Botrytis problems on some cultivars.

Gases. Flowers are sensitive to ethylene and will wilt after exposure to ethylene.

Lasting qualities. Cineraria will continue to flower for 4 to 6 weeks if they are kept at room temperatures of 55° to 60°F (13° to 16°C). Plants generally live 10 to 14 days in most home environments.

Care and grooming. Remove all dam-aged leaves and flowers before plants are sleeved and boxed. Be careful during sleeving to avoid breaking cineraria's large leaves and fragile flower stalks.

S

Senecio × hybridus

seh-*nee*-kee-oh
hye-brih-dus

Retail handling

Light. Place plants in a high light display area. Specific light levels have not been determined.

Temperature. Provide as cool a temperature as possible—55° to 60°F (13° to 16°C) is ideal to maintain plant quality.

Irrigation. Cineraria require large amounts of water. Thoroughly water plants and don't allow them to dry out.

Disorders. Major disorders are drying out, and insect and disease problems.

Consumer care

Light. Use interior light levels of 100 fc (1.1 klux) or more to maximize plant quality and flower development. Flowers that open at lower light levels are pale and irregularly colored, especially on the darker cultivars.

Temperature. Maintain 55°F (13°C) temperature for best longevity. Plants can be held at higher temperatures, but the lifespan will decrease. Placing plants on a 45° to 55°F (7° to 13°C) porch at night may increase longevity.

Location. Choose an east, south or west window to provide the light levels necessary for these plants.

Irrigation. Water plants thoroughly and frequently to avoid wilting and a shortened interior lifespan. Frequently plants that dry out indoors will not recover, even if the entire pot is submerged in water for a brief period to saturate the root system.

Grooming. Remove individual flowers as they fade. If lower leaves turn yellow, they can be removed without damaging the plant.

Disorders. Wilted plants: Failure to thoroughly water the plants on a frequent basis is a common problem on cineraria.

Faded flowers: Plants are generally sold with many unopened flower buds, which won't develop normal flower color if plants are placed at low interior light levels.

Cultivars. Cineraria seed sources provide only a mixed assortment of flower colors including reds, pinks, maroons, blues, oranges, whites and numerous bicolor variations. Generally, various shades of these colors are available within the assortment. No information is available on the longevity of specific cineraria varieties; however, major differences in longevity and interior performance exist among seed sources and colors within a seed line. Consider these factors in selecting cineraria varieties.

ADDITIONAL READING

Hammer, P.A. 1980. Other flowering potted plants. R.A. Larson, ed. *Introduction to Floriculture.* New York: Academic Press Inc.

Hildrum, H. 1969. Factors affecting flowering in Senecio crentus D.C. *Acta Horticultura* 14:117-123.

McDaniel, G.L. and G.L. Bresenham. 1978. Use of antitranspirants to improve water relations of cineraria. *HortScience* 13(4):466-467.

Sterling, E.P. and W.H. Molenaar. 1985. *Transport tolerantie van potplanten. Mededeling Nr. 39.* Wageningen, The Netherlands: Sprenger Institute.

Tu, Z.P., A.M. Armitage and H.M. Vines. 1985. Influence of an antitranspirant and a hydrogel on net photosynthesis and water loss of cineraria during water stress. *HortScience* 20(3):386-388.

S

Sinningia x *hybrida*

sin-*nin*-jee-uh
hye-brih-dah

Family Name: **Gesneriaceae**
Common Names: **Gloxinia, Sinningia**

Brazil—more than 75 species of perennial, hairy herbs or shrubs from Mexico to Argentina and Brazil. A small to large woody tuber is usually present.

LIBERTY BELLE

Production factors

No information is available on the effects of environmental production conditions or cultural practices on gloxinia interior longevity.

Stage of development. Plants are normally sold with four to six open flowers and the remaining buds showing color or visible. Proper interior conditions, as outlined below, are necessary for smaller buds to develop indoors.

Problems: Diseases: Crown rot, stem rot, root rot, black root rot, brown root rot and powdery mildew.

Insects: Red spider mites, cyclamen mites, loopers, army worms, mealybugs and thrips.

Disorder. Leaf spotting: Because leaves are sensitive to cold water, use irrigation water within 14°F (8°C) of air temperature to avoid this problem.

Postproduction factors

Shipping, handling and storage

Light. Gloxinias tolerate shipping for 3 days in a closed box at 60°F (16°C). The effects of extended shipping periods have not been identified specifically; however, long periods in the dark will lead to bud abortion.

Temperature. Ship plants at temperatures from 55° to 65°F (13° to 18°C). Because plants are cold-sensitive, temperatures below 50°F (10°C) will cause leaves and flowers to turn brown.

Lasting qualities. Plants continue to flower for 2 to 8 weeks.

Care and grooming. Gloxinias are difficult to sleeve without damaging the leaves. Shipping in trays without sleeves is suggested for local deliveries. Remove any damaged leaves and flowers before shipment.

S

Sinningia x hybrida

sin-*nin*-jee-uh
hye-brih-dah

Retail handling

Light. While gloxinias are tolerant of low light levels for brief periods, it's advisable to use 50 to 100 fc (.5 to 1.1 klux) of light during display. Placing plants in direct sunlight causes sunscald injury to leaves.

Temperature. Display plants at temperatures above 50°F (10°C) to avoid chilling injury. Display temperatures of 65° to 75°F (18° to 24°C) are preferred. Plants held at 65°F (18°C) will tolerate lower light levels and continue flowering longer than plants held at higher temperatures, unless the interior light level is increased above 100 fc (1.1 klux).

Irrigation. Keep plants uniformly moist, but don't overwater. Water on leaves may cause leaf spotting.

Disorder. Leaf spotting: Leaves become brown in areas where irrigation water that is more than 14°F (8°C) higher or lower than air temperature falls on leaves. Use of a capillary mat irrigation system in the display area is ideal to avoid foliage wetting.

Consumer care

Light. Low light (25 fc; 270 lux) is acceptable with cool temperatures (65°F; 18°C) but light levels of 50 to 100 fc (.5 to 1.1 klux) or higher are recommended for development of the greatest flower bud number. Avoid direct sunlight.

Temperature. Plants develop well at temperatures ranging from 65° to 75°F (18° to 24°C). Temperatures below 50°F (10°C) cause injury to leaves and flowers, while temperatures above 80°F (27°C) cause rapid flower opening, flower fading and possible bud abortion.

Location. Place plants near an east or south window.

Irrigation. Keep soil moist but not overwatered.

Grooming. Remove individual flowers as they die.

Disorder. Failure of flowers to open: Buds may fail to open if plants are not given sufficient light in the interior.

Cultivars. Excellent varieties are available offering numerous flower colors and either single or double blooms. No information regarding the longevity of gloxinia cultivars is currently available.

ADDITIONAL READING

Elliott, F.H. 1946. Saintpaulia leaf spot and temperature differential. *Proceedings of the American Society of Horticultural Science* 47:511-514.

Kimmins, R.K. 1980. Gloxinias, African violets, and other Gesneriads. R.A. Larson, ed. *Introduction to Floriculture*. New York: Academic Press.

Poesch, G.W. 1940. Tests show Saintpaulia ring spot caused by cold water. *Florists' Review* 87:21.

S

Streptocarpus × *hybridus*

strep-toh-*kar*-pus
hye-brih-dus

Family Name: **Gesneriaceae**
Common Name: **Cape Primrose**

Africa, Madagascar and Asia—about 132 species of often hairy, annual, perennial or monocarpic herbs or subshrubs.

THALIA

Production factors

No information is available on the effects of production practices or environmental conditions on the lifespan of streptocarpus.

Development stage. Market plants when 25% to 50% of the flowers are open, provided they are not being shipped. Plants with open flowers should be used only for local markets since flowers may drop during shipment. Use plants with three to six open flowers for orders requiring shipping.

Problems. Insect: Mealybugs.

Postproduction factors

Shipping, handling and storage

Light. Plants will tolerate darkness during shipping, provided shipping times do not exceed 6 days.

Temperature. Streptocarpus are sensitive to cool temperatures, so avoid temperatures below 50°F (10°C). Ship plants at 53° to 55°F (12° to 13°C) to minimize problems with ethylene.

Gases. Exposure to ethylene causes open flowers to wilt and drop during or following shipment. Apply silver thiosulfate (0.5 mM or less) 1 to 4 weeks prior to marketing to reduce flower abscission. Applications of silver thiosulfate 24 hours before shipping cause spotting of flowers and won't decrease flower drop.

Lasting qualities. Plants last 2 to 3 weeks or longer.

Care and grooming. Remove damaged or diseased leaves and flowers before shipping. Remove open flowers if plants are going to be shipped unless silver thiosulfate is bcing used.

Retail handling

Light. Display plants at light levels of 100 fc (1.1 klux).

S

Streptocarpus x *hybridus*

strep-toh-*kar*-pus
hye-brih-dus

Temperature. Provide temperatures from 65° to 80°F (18° to 27°C). Temperatures below 50°F (10°C) cause browning of flowers and foliage.

Irrigation. Keep plants moist but avoid overwatering.

Disorders. Flower and bud drop: This problem is a direct result of exposure to ethylene during shipping or display.

Leaf and flower browning: Chilling injury from exposure to temperatures below 50°F (10°C) causes browning of flowers and leaves.

Consumer care

Light. Provide a light level of 100 fc (1.1 klux) or greater to let small flower buds open indoors.

Temperature. Maintain temperatures between 70° to 75°F (21° to 24°C) for best results.

Location. Choose an east, south or west window, and avoid direct sunlight.

Irrigation. Keep plant moist at all times, but don't overwater.

Grooming. Remove old flowers and flower stalks.

Disorder. Failure of flowers and flower buds to open: This problem is most commonly caused by low light conditions, drying out or overwatering.

Cultivars. Plants are available with pink, red, purple, white, lilac and blue flowers. Differences in ethylene sensitivity and tolerance to low light conditions exist among the cultivars; however, no information is available on the longevity differences.

ADDITIONAL READING
Agnew, N.H., M.L. Lewnes and R.K. Kimmins. 1985. Reducing corolla abscission of *Streptocarpus* x *hybridus* under simulated shipping conditions with silver thiosulfate. *HortScience* 20:118-119.
Hammer, P.A. 1980. Other flowering plants. R.A. Larson, ed. *Introduction to Floriculture*. New York: Academic Press Inc.
Rewinkel-Jansen, M.J.H. 1985. Flower and bud abscission of streptocarpus and the use of ethylene sensitive inhibitors. *Acta Hoticultura* 181:419-423.

S

86

Flowering Potted Plants *Streptocarpus*

Tulipa spp.

tew-lip-uh

Family Name: **Liliaceae**
Common Name: **Tulip**

Central Asia—between 50 and 150 species of hardy spring-blooming bulbous perennial herbs. Most modern garden tulips are the result of extensive breeding and selection.

ORANGE MONARCH

Production factors

No information is available on the effects of production light level, temperature or media on tulip interior longevity.

Nutrition. Provide a nutritional program using calcium nitrate two to three times (2 pounds per 100 gallons; 907 g per 375 l) each week during forcing to minimize stem topple or collapse of the stem just below the flower.

Development stage. Market plants in the green bud stage to avoid injury during transport and maximize lifespan.

Problems. Diseases: Fusarium bulb rot, Penicillium, augusta virus, Rhizoctonia, Botrytis, viruses and Pythium.

Insects: Aphids.

Disorders. Stem topple: This problem—commonly observed on the cultivars Paul Richter, Elmus and Aureola—is promoted by numerous factors including forcing temperatures higher than 68°F (20°C), too many weeks of cold treatment and a lack of adequate calcium in the fertilizer program.

Flower abortion (blasting): Buds fail to develop to a marketable stage due to numerous factors including high forcing temperatures, exposure to ethylene, drying out during storage or forcing and poor ventilation during storage and transport.

Postproduction factors

Shipping, handling and storage

Light. Plants will withstand darkness during shipping or storage, but keep temperatures low to avoid excessive stem elongation and numerous physiological problems.

Temperature. Store and ship plants at 32° to 35°F (0° to 2°C).

Gases. Tulips are sensitive to ethylene, and exposure to ethylene will cause bud abortion.

Tulipa spp.   *tew*-lip-uh

Lasting qualities. Potted tulips last 1 to 2 weeks, depending on cultivar and interior conditions.

Care and grooming. Keep growing medium moist but not overly wet at the time of boxing.

Retail handling

Light. Light levels between 50 to 100 fc (.5 to 1.1 klux) have little effect on tulip longevity. Plants can be displayed at higher light levels without problems, but avoid direct light.

Temperature. Display tulips in a 60° to 68°F (16° to 20°C) area. Plants held at display temperatures above 70°F (21°C) will show rapid flower opening, stem topple and a loss of interior longevity.

Irrigation. Keep growing medium moist at all times, but avoid overwatering.

Disorder. Stem topple: See *Production factors*.

Flower abortion (blasting): See *Production factors*.

Consumer care

Light. Keep interior light level at 50 to 100 fc (1.1 klux) or higher.

Temperature. Plants are very responsive to interior temperature, with lifespan increasing by 7 days when plants are displayed at 65°F (18°C) compared to 80°F (27°C).

Location. Place plants in or near windows. Moving plants to a room providing 50° to 55°F (10° to 13°C) at night may extend plant's life.

Irrigation. Keep medium moist at all times.

Grooming. Remove faded flowers.

Cultivars. Many cultivars are forced as potted tulips. Tulips differ in lifespan, but specific information is not available regarding interior longevity of cultivars.

ADDITIONAL READING

De Hertogh, A.A. 1985. *Holland Bulb Forcers Guide.* New York: Netherlands Flower Bulb Institute.

Nell, T.A., A.A. De Hertogh and J.E. Barrett. 1991. Bulbs as flowering potted plants—keys to increased longevity. *GrowerTalks* 55(7):57-60.

T

Other flowering plant possibilities

There are a number of other flowering crops about which we have little or no specific information that are appropriate for potted plants. Some of these possibilities are listed below.

Abutilon sp.
Family name: Malvaceae
Common names: Flowering maple, parlor maple, Indian mallow
About 150 species of perennial herbs or soft, woody shrubs. Flowers are white, yellow, orange or reddish purple. Used as house plants and as bedding plants.

Achimenes sp.
Family name: Gesneriaceae
Common names: Monkey-faced pansy, orchid pansy, Japanese pansy, cupid's-bower
Approximately 26 species make up this group that is native to Jamaica, Mexico and Panama. Flowers can be solitary, in pairs or in cymes. Flower colors are violet with bicolors of red with yellow, violet with yellow or red with white.

Aeschynanthus sp.
Family name: Gesneriaceae
Common names: Basket plant, blushwort
A vine with deep red to scarlet, orange or greenish flowers. There are more than 100 species found in this genus from India and Southern China to New Guinea.

Allamanda cathartica, A. violacea
Family name: Apocynaceae
Common names: Golden trumpet, purple trumpet
A group of climbing shrubs with a milky sap that are native to tropical America. The funnel formed flowers are yellow or purple. Often grown on walls or fences.

Allium sp.
Family name: Amaryllidaceae
Common name: Onion
Over 400 species of strongly odorous herbaceous bulbs, primarily native to the Northern Hemisphere. Flowers are small, often found in umbels borne on a scape and subtended by a spathe. Several species are grown for food, while others are grown as ornamentals as a flower border in wild gardens or rock gardens.

Anemone sp.
Family name: Ranunculaceae
Common names: Windflower, lily-of-the-field
A group of perennial herbs with about 120 species native mostly to the north temperate zone. Flowers are often solitary with showy sepals ranging in color from yellow, white, rose or red to purple and violet. Used mainly in wild gardens.

Anthurium sp.
Family name: Araceae
Common name: Anthurium
A popular group of foliage plants that produce a colorful spathe. Plants do well under low light conditions, but high humidity is required for flowering. Both epiphytic and terrestrial species exist.

Browallia sp.
Family name: Solanaceae
Common name: Bush violet
About eight species of annual or perennial herbs native to tropical America. Flowers can be solitary or in a raceme. Plants are grown in the greenhouse and garden for the showy flowers, which are bluish purple with pale yellow eye, white to pale lilac, dark purple, blue, violet or white.

Other flowering plant possibilities

Caladium sp.
Family name: Araceae
Common names: Mother-in-law plant, elephant's-ear, angel-wings, caladium
Perennial herbs with colorful leaves that have a combination of red, white and green or other colors. Plants sprout from a tuber and have no stems.

Camellia japonica
Family name: Theaceae
Common name: Camellia
A group of evergreen small trees or shrubs from East Asia. For use primarily in mild climates, camellias are grown in shady outdoor areas. Flowers are single or sometimes double, in a variety of colors.

Cereus sp.
Family name: Cactaceae
Common name: Cereus
Includes about 36 species of ribbed cylindrical cacti that originated from the West Indies and Southeast America. Flowers bloom at night and are red, purple or white. This group does not include plants with the common name "night-blooming cereus," which are now in genera such as Hylocereus, Nyctocereus and Selenicereus.

Clivia sp.
Family name: Amaryllidaceae
Common name: Kaffir lily
Native to South Africa, this small group of herbaceous plants have flowers found in umbels. Flower color is reddish-yellow or scarlet. These are good plants for the greenhouse or indoor use.

Dahlia sp.
Family name: Compositae
Common name: Dahlia
A group of plants native to the mountains of Mexico, Central America and Colombia comprised of about 27 species of perennial herbs. The inflorescence is made up of disc and ray florets, and flower color ranges from white, yellow, orange and scarlet to purple.

Erica sp.
Family name: Ericaceae
Common name: Heather
Multibranched evergreen shrubs native to Europe, the Mediterranean and South Africa. Flowers are white, rose, purple, yellow or green, in a variety of shapes and sizes. They bloom in the winter and early spring. Some species are known to survive as far north as New York.

Fritillaria sp.
Family name: Liliaceae
Common name: Fritillaria
Spring-flowering herbaceous herbs native to Northwest America, Europe, Asia and North Africa. Inflorescences are terminal racemes or umbels, and individual flowers come in a variety of colors.

Fuchsia sp.
Family name: Onagraceae
Common name: Lady's-eardrops
A group of shrubs and trees that make up about 100 species of plants native from Mexico to Patagonia, New Zealand and Tahiti. Flowers are mostly showy, found in terminal racemes or panicles, in various shades of red to purple and white. These plants thrive under cool conditions and are grown outdoors in mild climates.

Other flowering plant possibilities

Galanthus sp.
Family name: Amaryllidaceae
Common name: Snowdrop
Spring-blooming bulbs native to Europe and Asia. Flowers are white and pendulous.

Gardenia sp.
Family name: Rubiaceae
Common name: Gardenia
Plants are shrubs or small trees that have a single fragrant flower of white or yellow color. They are grown indoors for cut flowers and outdoors in mild climates. Plants are produced in Europe and in the United States as flowering potted plants. Bud drop has been reported on potted plants following shipping and display in retail conditions.

Grevillea sp.
Family name: Proteaceae
Common name: Spider flower
About 250 species of evergreen shrubs and trees mostly native to Australia. Flowers are in a raceme or panicle inflorescence and are often brightly colored. Plants are grown as ornamental landscape trees in mild climates and occasionally as potted plants while young.

Jasminum sp.
Family name: Oleaceae
Common names: Jasmine, jessamine
Deciduous and evergreen shrubs, often climbing, native to Asia, Africa and Australia. Flowers are white, yellow or pink and sometimes fragrant. They are grown outdoors in warm climates and as potted plants in other regions.

Justicia sp.
Family name: Acanthaceae
Common names: Jacobinia, water willow
Herbaceous perennials native to the tropics and subtropics. Flowers are in a cyme, spike or panicle inflorescence with colors ranging from white to red or purple.

Kohleria sp.
Family name: Gesneriaceae
Common name: Tree gloxinia
A group of more than 50 species of herbs or shrubs native to Mexico and South America. Flowers are solitary or in a raceme, and flower color can be rose and purple-red, yellow and purple, purple, orange-yellow or lavender-violet.

Lantana sp.
Family name: Verbenaceae
Common names: Lantana, shrub verbena
About 150 species of prickly shrubs or perennial herbs native to subtropical and tropical North and South America. Flowers come in various colors. These plants are used in the landscape in mild climates, and one species is commonly used in floral arrangements.

Leucojum sp.
Family name: Amaryllidaceae
Common name: Snowflake
Small herbaceous bulbs native to Europe with leaves that arise from the plant's base. Flowers are white, tinged with yellow, red or green and are on a scape.

Other flowering plant possibilities

Lilium hybrids
Family name: Liliaceae
Common name: Asiatic lily
This group of hybrid lilies is native to China. They are derived from such species or hybrid groups as *L. tigrinum, L. cernuum, L. davidii, L. leichtlinii, L. x maculatum, L. x hollandicum, L. amabile, L. pumilum, L. concolor* and *L. bulbiferum.*
Family name: Liliaceae
Common name: Oriental lily
This group of hybrid lilies is native to Japan. They are derived from species such as *L. auratum, L. speciosum, L. japonicum, L. rubellum* and *L. henryi.*

Puschkinia scilloides
Family name: Liliaceae
Common name: Puschkinia
Spring-blooming herbaceous bulbs native to Asia Minor and the Caucasus. Leaves arise from the base, and white flowers are in a raceme on a scape.

Scilla sp.
Family name: Liliaceae
Common name: Scilla
A group of about 80 to 90 species of perennial herbaceous bulbs native to Africa, Europe and Asia. Flowers are blue to purple or white in a raceme inflorescence. Grown outdoors and in cool greenhouses, bulbs can be left undisturbed for many years. Natural flowering time is early spring.

Torenia sp.
Family name: Scrophulariaceae
Common names: Wishbone flower, wishbone plant
This genus is made up of about 40 annual or perennial herbs from tropic and subtropic Asia and Africa. Flowers are simple with various colors in terminal racemes.

Zantedeschia sp.
Family name: Araceae
Common name: Calla lily
A small group of stemless herbs native to South Africa. These plants are known for their showy spathe, which can be white, pale yellow with a purple throat, yellow, or white with rose spots. Calla lilies are grown outdoors in mild climates and often in greenhouses.

GLOSSARY

Abscission. Dropping of buds, leaves or flowers. Numerous mechanical and physiological factors may cause this problem.

Auxin. Class of plant growth regulators.

Cultivar. A horticultural variety.

Cyathium (cyathia). Relatively inconspicuous flowers on plants having showy bracts, such as poinsettia and bougainvillea.

Cytokinin. Class of plant growth regulators.

Epinasty. A downward bending or droop of leaves and bracts caused by a hormonal imbalance. In poinsettia, petioles, leaves and bracts droop after plants have been sleeved. Plants will generally recover within 24 hours.

Ethylene. An odorless, colorless gas that acts as a plant growth regulator. Exposure to ethylene generally reduces longevity and has numerous negative effects on flowering potted plants, such as leaf and bud drop.

GA. Gibberellin, a class of plant growth regulators.

Hormone. A plant growth regulator produced by the plant.

Leaf/bract droop. See Epinasty.

Leaf scorch. Browning of leaves caused by fluoride toxicity in lilies and water stress, overfertilization or pesticide phytotoxicity in other crops.

Longevity. Postproduction period during which a flowering potted plant meets the consumer's aesthetic expectations of the crop.

Marketability. The state of horticultural maturity (stage of development) at which flowering potted plants can be sold.

Necrosis. Darkening of leaf/bract tissue caused by death of cells. Injury is generally on leaf margins or bracts.

Phylloclad. Flattened leaf structures as in Christmas and Easter cactus.

Precooling. A procedure to rapidly cool plants or flowers prior to shipping.

pH. The measure of acidity or alkalinity, from 0 to 14. A pH of 7.0 is neutral, below 7.0 is acid and above 7.0 is alkaline. Close to a pH of 0 is very acid, close to 14 is very alkaline.

Plant growth regulator. A substance that has an effect on plant growth or development.

ppm. Parts per million. A unit of measure used in preparing chemical concentrations.

Quality. A term that represents the appearance and/or value of a flowering potted plant including size, shape, freedom from mechanical, insect and disease injury, and flower color.

Stage of development. See Marketability.

STS. Silver thiosulfate, inhibitor of ethylene action. Usually used at a concentration of about 1 to 4 millimolar (mM).

CROP INDEX

CROP INDEX